PRAISE FOR
EVERYDAY COMMUNICATION STRATEGIES

'This is a first-class issues management book. Informed and authoritative, this step-by-step guide is packed with examples and exercises. Practitioners should keep it by their side and read it repeatedly.'
Anne Gregory, Emeritus Professor of Corporate Communication, University of Huddersfield

'The book you are holding is a real masterpiece and a precise guide on communicating professionally in the modern world. Amanda Coleman expertly structures her messages and makes each sentence of this book invaluable. It advises you on boosting your business as well as preventing a communications crisis. When you close the last page of the book, you will keep it on your desk or bedside as a daily consultant in your business.'
Maxim Behar, CEO, M3 Communications Group, Inc and President, World Communication Forum Association

'Amanda Coleman has lived and breathed issues management throughout her professional life. This excellent and detailed book is both comprehensive and enormously helpful. It provides a great step-by-step approach to managing the issues communicators face every day in their roles – and making sure that they do not blow up into something more serious.'
Jim Donaldson, CEO UK and Middle East, FleishmanHillard UK

'An excellent follow up to her outstanding book *Crisis Communication Strategies*. Amanda Coleman provides an indispensable guide for public relations and communications pros on the best practices for handling issues and decision making to avoid the crisis stage.

I encourage both novices and old hats to add this book to their practice!'

Bob Jensen, Senior Managing Director, Strat3, former Principal Deputy Assistant Secretary, US Department of Homeland Security and White House spokesperson

'One of the most useful books on the subject and it is great to see Amanda Coleman cast her expert eye over issues management. This is a compendium of valuable and constructive advice on how to prepare for and deal with issues from an organizational perspective and, in doing so, prevent crises and protect reputations and relationships. It is full of top tips and relevant case studies. I found the sections on messaging, team structures and decision making under pressure particularly useful.'

Ben Verinder, reputation research agency owner and lead assessor for Chartered PR status

'Skilful PR is vital in a crisis, but requires being prepared, with thorough plans and strategies in place. Critically though, it also plays a key role in avoiding that crisis in the first place. In this authoritative book, Amanda Coleman sets out a common-sense and comprehensive approach to issues management, providing outstanding guidance that will be relevant to everyone in our industry. A must-read for anyone working in reputation management.'

Francis Ingham MPRCA, Director General, PRCA and Chief Executive, ICCO

'Amanda Coleman's book is an essential manual for reputation management in times of constant crises. Providing a 360-degree overview on current crisis trends and real-life examples on possible crisis scenarios, this book will help you rewrite your crisis plan and protect your reputation in a polarized world.'

Kosta Petrov, Founder and Managing Director, P World

Everyday Communication Strategies

Manage common issues to prevent a crisis and protect your brand

Amanda Coleman

KoganPage

First published in Great Britain and the United States in 2023 by Kogan Page Limited

2nd Floor, 45 Gee Street	8 W 38th Street, Suite 902	4737/23 Ansari Road
London	New York, NY 10018	Daryaganj
EC1V 3RS	USA	New Delhi 110002
United Kingdom		India
www.koganpage.com		

Kogan Page books are printed on paper from sustainable forests.

ISBNs

Hardback   978 1 3986 0699 9
Paperback   978 1 3986 0697 5
Ebook   978 1 3986 0698 2

British Library Cataloguing-in-Publication Data
A CIP record for this book is available from the British Library.

Library of Congress Control Number
2022035604

Typeset by Hong Kong FIVE Workshop
Print production managed by Jellyfish
Printed and bound by CPI Group (UK) Ltd, Croydon CR0 4YY

*This book is dedicated to my Mum – Prue – who sadly died as
I was completing it. Artist, creative thinker, gardener, philosopher,
animal lover and much more, she was the most amazing woman
and a force of nature. Her belief in me and insistence that you can
achieve anything if you really want it has been a constant support.
I will be forever grateful for everything that my Mum has given me,
and I know she will be a guiding light in my future.*

*A huge thank you to my Dad – Philip – and my partner Jonathan,
who have been a great support even as we dealt with
the darkest moments. Finally, the two four-legged companions who
bring joy into my life – Edward the horse and Digger the rabbit.
Thank you for being there when I needed you the most.*

CONTENTS

ABOUT THE AUTHOR

Amanda Coleman is a PR and communication professional with many years' experience of managing issues, incidents and crises. Her first book *Crisis Communication Strategies* was published by Kogan Page in May 2020. Amanda is a Fellow of both the Chartered Institute of Public Relations and the Public Relations and Communications Association, as well as being a Chartered PR Practitioner.

Amanda runs a crisis, risk and reputation communication consultancy and works with public and private sector organizations to prepare for and respond to challenging situations. She is Chair of the Emergency Planning Society Communication Professional Working Group, an adviser with the Resilience Advisors Network, and a senior associate with the Centre of Crisis and Risk Communication.

PREFACE

When I wrote my first book *Crisis Communication Strategies* it made me realize there was an important piece of PR and communication work that I had not covered. I had not talked about the bit that happens before the crisis emerges. The time when there is a murmur of a problem, a hint of an issue or a minor incident taking place. I had assumed that we were always dealing with a full-blown crisis. But if we get issues management right, then we can hopefully avoid heading into a crisis that threatens to damage a business. So, consider this book a prequel to *Crisis Communication Strategies* that looks at those everyday situations all communicators face. I hope that people find it useful in assessing what they do and looking at how they can more effectively deal with day-to-day decision making.

Each day communicators and PR professionals make decisions about what to do: how to promote that latest development, how to keep employees informed, how to connect to customers. With each of these decisions comes the pressure to perform and make the right decision. This book aims to give some tips, techniques and approaches that will help you to make that 'right decision' more of the time. Being more effective in issues management starts with the right monitoring system, one that will alert to any potential challenges that are emerging. Getting that right is not as simple as it may seem, with the proliferation of social media channels putting considerable demands on the communicator and their response.

Before you are even aware that an issue has emerged there also needs to be a clear structure, framework and governance system in place to help you, and the business, through what is happening. Issues management has long been seen as of less significance than crisis communication. Some may feel they do it every day so why does there need to be training, planning and consultation in place to address things? We all face issues to deal with every day but are we making it harder for ourselves than we need to, and could there be more effective ways of approaching these situations? I hope that through this book people will find ways they can become more effective and halt the escalation of issues into crises.

The way we approach social media and the news media underpins the work to manage issues. We have to use our daily interactions and activities to put us in the right place when a problem develops. If we know journalists and how they work, and if we understand the connections we have through social media, then we are in a stronger position. When an issue emerges, it is not the time to have to develop all these things; we need to have done the hard work so that we can quickly intervene and find a way to reach a solution. Problem solving has always been part of the communicator's role and I know from experience that the right approach in the initial stages can prevent an issue escalating. Communicators have a key role to play in issues management, risk reduction and crisis planning within an organization. This includes helping the rest of the business to be trained and ready to intervene to stop the problem in its tracks.

At the centre of all issues and incident management is effective decision making and taking an ethical approach to the work; this is why I have devoted two chapters to exploring these key areas. Communicators and PR professionals talk a lot about ethics and ethical communication and with issue management there is the chance to put the theory into practice. There should never be an attempt to mislead or undermine people who have genuine complaints or concerns about the business. Gaslighting must be avoided. After more than 20 years working in police communication, I have seen the damage that can be done by a few ill-chosen words, or a failure to see the problem that people were alerting you to.

Issues management is not, and should not be seen as, a negative situation. It represents a huge opportunity for a business to learn and develop, but first it has to be willing to listen. This book aims to provide the starting point to review current working arrangements but also to identify what role risk and issues management plays in day-to-day communication activity. I have also provided case studies to spark discussion and debate, and a series of exercises in Chapter 9 for you or your team to work through. Beyond that there are ways to hone your understanding and management of issues through introducing some simple daily tasks. I hope some of these are, or can be, added to the way you operate.

Every single business, organization, CEO and communication professional needs to understand issues management and be ready to deal with problems that occur. Unlike the once-in-a-career crisis situation, issues are something we will all face regularly in our working lives. Getting the response right can make us stronger as professionals and businesses.

ACKNOWLEDGEMENTS

Bringing this book together would not have been possible without the support of many people both in communication and issues planning roles. I am grateful for the support I have received from both the Chartered Institute of Public Relations and the Public Relations and Communications Association. Thank you to everyone I have spoken to in researching the book. Every conversation has helped me to shape what I have included. A special thank you to Victoria Poole and the Education Authority in Northern Ireland, and Keith Wilson and Hampshire and Isle of Wight Air Ambulance. Finally, to the team at Kogan Page, who have helped me stay on track, particularly Heather Wood, who has shown endless patience.

1

What is issues management?

Introduction

Every day there are problems that communicators face and have to deal with. Events and issues emerge and can threaten the reputation, market position and operation of the business. Such situations are just part of the challenges of running any organization or business. Issues fill the pages of the newspapers, and feature in TV and radio news broadcasts. They are what is trending on social media and what gets talked about when people meet in the street. Issues are part of life but that does not mean they have to be allowed to run out of control and cannot be carefully managed to secure an effective outcome. But achieving this requires communicators to take a fresh look at the work they do when they are not facing any issues and are simply conducting normal day-to-day business. Reflecting, reviewing, and reconsidering the approach that they take every day can improve the response, save money and time, and leave the business in a stronger position when problems emerge.

When talking about issues and incidents it is important to be clear what they are, and what they are made up of. Put simply, these are the negative and challenging moments that threaten the smooth operation of the organization. They are the times when something goes wrong, whether that is a bad review on social media, an employee behaving inappropriately, or a product or system failing. Managing these situations well will build confidence from both within and outside the organization. Employees and particularly managers will see how strategic and tactical communication activities work together to achieve positive results. At the same time customers, people using the product or service, and stakeholders will be kept informed and have a clear understanding of the situation that has arisen. These incidents are not on the same scale as a crisis, but they do require the same careful thought and consideration. Unlike a crisis situation these moments appear more frequently and test us on a regular basis. Despite the fact that we are more familiar with these events they still require thought and planning if they are to be effectively dealt with.

Public relations practitioners spend their time each day focused on building reputation and brand awareness. They are looking for proactive opportunities to support their client or organization using a whole variety of channels and methods of communication. But all of this work can be undone or damaged by a poor response to any number of low-level issues. Where possible these situations, often seen as minor problems, should be contained, and managed quickly. But where that is not possible it is essential to carefully work through the storm to get to the rainbow. It is vital that strategies are put in place that can help the organization navigate its way through the situation. Speed and action are two elements that are fundamental to the management of issues and incidents; an effective response cannot happen without both of them being in play. More than that, communicators can get ahead of the problem by looking at how and when they may need to respond to issues and what follow-up action may be required to prevent the situation from re-emerging at some point in the future. The starting point for all such situations is to spot what is happening and then put in place measures to deal with it. There are a range of ways to respond to a challenging issue, and these will be covered in subsequent chapters.

Issues and reputation

Building a reputation is helped when the business has an effective incident management process with communication operating at the heart of it. But trust and confidence can be quickly damaged when the words used do not match the organization's actions. People quickly become cynical when the response the business puts in place varies from, or is at odds with, what is being said. It is important if this situation is developing for someone to challenge what is happening. Communicators face a range of ethical dilemmas when an issue emerges within a business. This could be anything from a failure to recognize the situation that is developing from across the business, to active denial of the problem by the executive team. It may even be attempts by senior staff to manipulate and coerce in relation to the situation. To tackle this, it may be necessary for communicators to step outside their comfort zone and the traditional boundaries of communication and PR activity in order that the full implications of the situation are understood and addressed. They may need to challenge, to call out bad behaviour, or to suggest another course of action. Remember that any incident will be a reflection of an organization's culture and values and people will be watching to see the action that is taken. Failure by any business to see the full picture can be damaging both at the moment the issue emerges and at points in the future.

There is a phenomenon known as the butterfly effect,[1] where small changes at one point can have a major impact many miles away. The same can be seen in dealing with issues and incidents. What may appear to be a minor problem or a small blip in the operation of the business could become much more serious either to the business itself at some point in the future or to other individuals, businesses, situations, or locations. In reverse, looking at how to respond, failure to act can also have an effect on the business. It is why it is so critical to consider how, when and in what ways you will respond to issues. It ensures you can develop the most effective response and be able to focus on the small things that make a big difference.

It is important to recognize that these issues and incidents do not fit the criteria of being a crisis for the organization or business. A crisis has to be a much more serious and critical point in time or an emergency situation. It will involve the whole organization, is potentially life-threatening or damaging to property, and it endangers the very operation of the business. Issues and incidents may never be severe enough to become crises but can over time seriously damage the reputation of the business and people's confidence in it. This makes an effective response and communication critical to ensuring problems don't have a negative impact.

Defining the problem

Before embarking on a discussion about issues, incidents, and problems there needs to be a clear understanding of what each of them is and what they mean. It is also important to understand what factors are in place when they happen and are classified as serious to the business. In a nutshell, issues, incidents and problems are all linked, and the terms can be, and are, used interchangeably in many organizations. However, the way you define things matters only to you and the business. There needs to be a shared language within the business so that people understand what is meant when talking about issues, incidents and problems. Clear definitions of critical incidents and issues have happened in some sectors of business and can be seen in sectors such as law enforcement, health, and education.

An issue is defined as 'an important topic or problem for debate or discussion'.[2] In this case something does not have to physically happen, as it can be related to planning, the operation of processes, positioning or development that leads to potentially damaging exchanges. In contrast, an incident is when something has happened or occurred that could create a problem for the business. There is some physically tangible aspect in place when an incident occurs. It is important to note the differences between issues and incidents when you start to consider how to approach them and the responses that may be required from a communication perspective. At the heart of all these is the recognition that there is some form of problem, and it is negative or potentially negative for the organization. This does not mean that organizations cannot find opportunities for positivity within the response, but the situation has to be very carefully managed.

Issues management exists at the centre of the PR professional's world and for many years it has been seen as a mainstay of the work undertaken. However, issues management is often confused or conflated into crisis management. It is important to understand the threshold that exists that moves something from being an issue or incident within the business into a crisis. This may exist through an unwritten understanding among managers and employees but can, and should, be documented to ensure there is clarity for all. Issues management can also be mistaken for reputation management but the two are not the same. Reputation management is how you influence people's views of an organization, business, or brand. It can be both reactive and proactive. There does not need to be a direct link from reputation to issues and incident management, and this will be explored in more detail in Chapter 3.

More than reputation

The reality is that issues management is about identifying and responding to emerging trends and changes, as well as other elements that may affect the daily operation and the long-term goals of the business. Dealing with these issues is not only about protecting reputation but covers so much more, including ensuring the smooth running of the business, project, or initiative.

As mentioned, in some professions there are clear definitions and processes for the management of what are often called 'critical incidents'. Within education it is 'An event or sequence of events affecting pupils and/or staff which creates significant personal distress to a level which potentially overwhelms normal responses, procedures and coping strategies and which is likely to have serious emotional and organizational consequences.'[3]

The definition keeps the focus on the impact of the events and the potential for the situation to derail or prevent education activity taking place. Within this definition the emotional consequences are given a central position. This can help to focus the priorities, actions and evaluation of the event or issue and keep people at the heart of the activity.

Within the UK National Health Service, the approach towards critical incidents is focused on the failure of internal systems, activities, or procedures and is defined as 'an incident that occurred in relation to NHS-funded services and care resulting in unexpected or avoidable death, harm or injury to patient, carer, staff or visitor.'[4]

They are often referred to as serious or critical incidents and will have clear structures around the reporting and management of them. Again, this definition is centred around the human elements and the impact on the people who are caught up in the incident.

For policing in the UK, the College of Policing has developed the Authorised Professional Practice, which defines a critical incident as 'any incident where the effectiveness of the police response is likely to have a significant impact on the confidence of the victim, their family and/or the community'.[5]

The definition brings together the operational failings with recognition that they have had an impact on people. However, this definition in itself can be open to misinterpretation when it moves out of balance and the priority becomes the management of the organization's reputation.

There is more to each of these three approaches than just the definition of a critical incident; the real strength comes from the structures and frameworks that are in place to support the response – this will be discussed in Chapter 2. These professions have clear and widely understood definitions and approaches to critical incident management because of the high level of risk that they carry. There is an increased likelihood that any of these incidents could quickly become a crisis for the organization.

TOP TIP

Develop a shared understanding of how to categorize situations that emerge and can affect the operation of the business. This means putting in place agreements about the threshold where a situation becomes an issue that needs to be addressed, and also when it moves from being an issue to becoming a crisis. Determining the appetite for risk and where risk management is placed within the business can assist in developing these agreed definitions.

What makes an issue?

Issues and incidents come from problems and situations that can negatively impact on the business. The potential for this exists when a range of circumstances come together, and can develop to become a major concern. For these issues to develop a number of elements will be involved. It is important to understand what these are as it helps in the identification of issues and incidents as well as developing an early intervention to work towards a positive outcome. When events occur, these elements are triggered and can build to create the issue. It is like joining the points to create a circuit that allows the problem to emerge as the energy flows between these points. Each connection that is made helps to develop the circuit or in this case the creation of an issue that may impact on the business. They do not all need to be in place but with enough of them, and with enough intensity, it can complete that circuit. Managing the situation will break this circuit so that it cannot develop into a serious issue. Each strategy that is put in place and each action that is taken can help to ensure the circuit is not created. This is why action needs to be taken to prevent issues developing.

There are eight elements that may be involved in the development of an issue. The situation will have all or some of these elements if it is going to become a problem for an organization or business:

1 It is an unexpected situation for the brand or business.

2 The situation is negatively impacting on the business's reputation.

3 People and/or property are affected.

4 The impact of it is seen or heard by someone.

5 It is newsworthy.

6 There is a misunderstanding.

7 People may be concerned, upset, or offended.

8 There is a perceived injustice.

It is unexpected

The business did not expect the issue would arise. Even if it had been identified as part of the risk management process it was not rated highly on the likelihood that it would occur. The situation emerges or develops with little notice. The situation may have been developing out of sight and monitoring has not picked it up. People are also likely to be surprised that the brand or organization is involved in this kind of issue or incident. This creates a feeling that something has gone wrong or is not as it should be.

It is negative

The issue or incident will have a negative impact, or a potential negative impact, on the reputation of the brand or organization. Whatever the situation is that is developing it will continue to be negative unless it is recognized, and a decision is taken about the next steps. This is why early identification of issues is essential as it allows additional time to put communication plans and actions into place.

It has affected people/property

When considering issues, it is important to understand who or what is, or may be, affected by what is developing. If there is no significant impact on people or property, then the situation is unlikely to demand the same level of response. The impact of the issue may be direct or indirect, which is why this element needs careful consideration. For example, a critical review of the business or product will mean there is an unhappy customer, and in the case of online trolling it will impact on those being targeted.

It is seen or heard

Whether it is on social media, in the media, or through word of mouth, people will have identified the impact of the issue. It will be the subject of discussion and debate, and when the conversation about it grows, the problem will become more serious. Before it becomes public, the issue is just a problem that is waiting to happen. The moment it is seen and heard by people it means it is about to grow and become more challenging for the business.

It is newsworthy

This links closely with the fact that it is an unexpected situation for the brand or business and people and/or property have been affected. This means the issue is of interest to journalists, bloggers, and commentators. Once this has happened then the issue is going to require immediate attention and definite action. This, connected to the fact that people are talking about it, starts to make the connections to complete the circuit.

It is a misunderstanding

The issue involves a lack of clarity about a situation which has then developed into a misunderstanding. For example, an organization may make a change to a product or service without fully communicating what is going to take place. People will then learn about it from unreliable sources or will only have partial information, which may mean they perceive the situation in a negative way. The day-to-day communication that is undertaken by organizations can be one of the best ways to mitigate the development of issues provided this communication is effective, clear, and easy to understand.

It can create concern, upset or offence

When a situation impacts on people and this impact is negative, as mentioned earlier, then it can develop to cause concern, upset or offence. If this happens then it will increase the discussion and conversations taking place about the issue, which will intensify the spotlight on what has happened. When people are unhappy or upset about something, they are more likely to comment on it negatively. This will put further pressure on the organization or brand. Again, the circuit is being created for an issue to emerge.

It is a perceived injustice

When a situation develops and it is felt there has been, or will be, an injustice, this again is leading to a serious issue. If it involves a big organization set against a member of the public, this creates a David and Goliath situation which attracts additional attention. People like to see the underdog succeed when they have been put in a difficult situation by corporations. The media also focus on the struggle between individuals and faceless corporate bodies. This will challenge the brand or business to be sensitive to the situation that has emerged but also to the perception that people have, if they are to achieve a positive outcome. The issue of injustice and its impact will be considered further in Chapter 3.

Politically driven issues

There are occasions where an issue facing a business is being driven by politics. Public sector organizations can find they are at the centre of a problem created and developed through political interventions, and businesses may see a development or change hijacked for some political gains. If the organization is in a sensitive, controversial or high-profile sector it is likely to attract a lot of external interest. This may lead to briefings in political circles and in the worst case counter-briefing when others pass comment and share views in an attempt to undermine your position. Being aware of the potential for these situations to happen is important. But more than that you will need to carefully consider what actions you take, particularly when you cannot disagree publicly for whatever reason.

As we will cover, stakeholder mapping is crucial to identify any political links and to understand the network that the business operates within. This highlights where relationships need to be fostered and developed. However, even with strong relationships there will be occasions when politicians have a different perspective on what the business is doing. Being aware of the approach they may take and what it means to your response to the issue is a crucial first step. Politicians both local and national can also turn a minor situation into a significant issue by increasing the interest in what has happened from the public, the media and other political leaders. This will create a politically driven issue that develops into a problem despite the work the business has undertaken to manage it.

Identifying an issue

The identification of an issue can happen too late to be able to intervene and put mitigation in place to limit its impact. By the time communicators become aware, the problem is already starting to grow and to be featured both in the media and on social media. People will be talking about it and will be watching to see what develops. At this point the issue will be impacting on the operation of the business and has the potential to be detrimental to confidence in the organization. For example, if there is a problem with a product, people will be discussing it online and sales may fall. In order to allow early intervention and then put measures in place to prevent escalation the issue needs to be identified swiftly. The longer the delay in recognizing that something is happening, the more likely it is that the situation will become more challenging for the organization and its operation. It is also more likely that it will cause damage. Delays in identifying the issue give rumours time to spread and failures in the business are allowed to grow, making the job of the communicator harder when attempting to reach a satisfactory conclusion. Being able to identify issues at the moment they emerge is therefore essential to effective management of issues and incidents. It means there can be swift intervention to prevent any escalation and the deployment of communication activities to start to turn things around. When issues and incidents grow unchecked, they will quickly start to take limited resources away from other important pieces of work.

Highlighting an emerging issue is about more than allowing effective communication to take place. Recognizing what is starting to occur can help to ensure the smooth running of the business through early intervention. For example, if you have a critical online review of a product or service there may be key points of that feedback that need to be taken up to change and develop the product or service. It may even highlight where a product needs to be recalled because of manufacturing problems. If you fail to see and read these negative comments, then more customers may be affected by the same issue, leading to growing numbers of unhappy customers and allowing the problem to gather momentum. This may impact on the operation of the business, affecting sales, hindering developments, and damaging reputation.

Developing an issues mindset

Being in a position to identify a situation early will increase the likelihood of a more successful conclusion. There is an opportunity to understand what the problem is and, beyond that, the issues surrounding it. Environmental factors can change the way communication should be focused. A prevailing mood or tone about the problem needs to be understood and used to inform the communication. With early identification there is more time to develop the response, to create escalation plans and manage interventions. Where it starts is looking at trends, developments, and changes that may affect the operation of the business. Knowing these will help the identification of issues and incidents at an early stage, supporting a swift response.

To be able to identify issues requires a change in the mindset of communicators and key leaders and managers within the business. The role of communication must be allowed to expand so that it operates both strategically and tactically within the business. Communication is not just about sending out news releases, organizing photo calls, or producing content. Communication should be working as an arm of the business operation, alongside product development or service delivery. The organization needs to allow the space for people to develop into this role, and the communication team need to support the change by stepping up and understanding the detailed operation of the business. In doing this, communication can start to demonstrate a direct impact on the bottom line of the business. This is only possible if there is an approach that sees wider than promotion, reputation management and brand development.

Six areas where issues happen

A communicator looking at how to identify issues and where to start can consider six aspects of the business operation. These six main areas are where issues can emerge: people, product, policies, perceptions, finances, and environment. Each of these are fundamental pillars of the business strategy and will be where issues and incidents occur. People, both staff and customers, may do or say things that can create an issue, or increase the intensity of an issue. Examples of issues involving people can be customer complaints or staff discontentment with a decision or course of action. Issues involving products are often linked to product changes, developments, or failures in some way. Policy issues emerge when an organization or business adopts an approach to something that may be controversial, misunderstood or a problem. Perceptions lead to issues on many occasions as they are based on people having a view about the business that may not be accurate or correct. Finances are where issues lurk, with concerns about how money is spent, what things cost, or the pay of senior executives. Finally, the environmental factors are those that occur around the business but not within its direct operation. For example, there may be a breakdown in a logistics chain that the business gets caught up in, or a product contamination at a competitor might create concerns for other businesses. Consideration of these aspects of the business operation will assist the communicator in recognizing that an issue is emerging.

Where do issues come from?

The reality is that issues can emerge from any part of the organization and things that are around it. This may seem like a major problem for communicators who can feel stretched because of limited resources and an unlimited possibility of issues. They may struggle to monitor and assess everything to identify issues. However, there are many ways to be ready to spot an issue and these can be built into the everyday communication and PR operation within an organization or business. Issues management should not be seen as an additional burden or extra piece of work to add to a long 'to do' list but instead should be part of an effective communication operation. The starting point for communicators is to be alert. Be aware of how issues and incidents can and do develop and be ready to act swiftly. When you are working with, or in, the same organization for a long time it brings huge benefits as you know a lot about how it functions, where problems may come from, and the key people to involve. But it is easy to switch off your antenna and not be vigilant to emerging situations. Communicators can become blinkered or start to expect the things that have always happened because they have a long history to draw upon. To banish this the communicator must develop their own skills and build systems into their everyday work that will support fresh thinking and decision making. This will be covered in Chapter 7.

Listening carefully

Listening is a way of being able to look at situations from a different perspective or to understand if the elements of the circuit mentioned earlier are coming into play. This means really listening. It may be listening to differing views, listening to concerns, listening to discussions about developments, listening to feedback, or listening to criticism. When communicators are busy with the daily work of promoting a business and developing brand awareness, they can become focused on their view of the world at the expense of recognizing events happening around it. Using data and insights is essential to provide vital information but there is always a place for conversations that can inform and highlight issues. It is why communication should always involve people outside the PR and communication team. Diversity of opinion and thought is needed to create effective communication. Customer focus groups, stakeholder engagement events and employee forums are all ways that you can both listen to and involve people in the development of the business. Alongside this positive work, such groups can also be a way to gather intelligence and information about any current or future issues. Listening to key groups is one way that you can seamlessly introduce issue management processes into everyday communication work. These groups may already exist; they just need to be connected into the communication function of the business.

Business knowledge

Communicators must know the business in detail, from the way the product or service is created through to the vision for development over the next five or ten years. They need to know where the money is spent, what the financials look like, where the assets are and any financial risks. They need to know why people join and why people leave. They need to know who the key stakeholders are and who is interested in what they do. In short, if communicators are going to be able to promote and maximize the opportunities to build the brand, they must have a thorough understanding of the business they are supporting. This is fundamental to everyday communication but is also critical to issue and incident identification and subsequent interventions and management of the situation. It is important to understand what the usual is and what it looks like, and what is unusual. Consider what developments are expected and look at what it means if the unexpected happens. It is those unusual situations that will again trigger a connection in the circuit towards creating an issue.

Change management has a direct impact on issues management processes. People find change unsettling and this can often be the start of where misunderstandings can occur, which in turn will start to trigger the emergence of an issue. Having clarity about the changes that are taking place, where the impact will be and where the risks may occur, is central to issues identification. For example, if you work for a soft drinks company and you change your recipe or flavour without explanation or a conversation with consumers, it may prompt a negative response. Or it may be a local hospital or doctor that changes the process to make appointments; if this has not been appropriately communicated to patients an issue will develop. The changes may improve the service or product but without clarity in communication and explanation, and consideration of those who dislike change, it will become a negative position where issues management has to take over. This emphasizes the importance of having communication representation involved in the decision-making process, meetings or body based within a business or organization. It will allow early recognition of issues that may occur when decisions are made; this can inform the debate and discussion, as well as allow the development of strategies to address those issues.

Commentary

Issues will also get people with differences of opinion talking about the situation. This polarization will fuel the conversation and as that develops so can the negative impact of the issue on the reputation of the organization. More people talking about it means it is likely to start trending on social media and be picked up by the traditional media. Once that happens the issue will become critical and pressure will grow on the business to show decisive action. Careful monitoring of commentary about the business on social media is an essential part of the identification process. Just one comment can be a warning that a problem is developing. If this leads to further comments, then it is clear an issue is emerging and a move to intervention must take place. Similarly, once a local reporter has contacted the business about a comment in relation to a change, development or subject, then care needs to be taken in crafting the response to prevent any further issues. As we will see in Chapter 2, the structures and frameworks put in place around the management of communication and issues are critical to early identification and a swift move to a satisfactory outcome. The communication professional needs to have a sphere of influence that will put them at the heart of the development of the business and also the management of issues, incidents, and problems.

TOP TIP

Always analyse the situation so that you understand where it has come from, what has caused it to develop, and what impact it has already had before any action has been taken. This will give you a strong foundation on which to develop the strategy to respond. Data and insight, both qualitative and quantitative, will help this analysis.

The role of the communicator

Issues management needs communication to be a key strand of how the business responds in a proactive way. There is no room for passive communication and communicators when you are dealing with a problem. If communication is brought in at the last minute to write a news statement, then moving to a satisfactory outcome will be a lottery. You may succeed but you will be leaving things to chance. With some luck there will be another situation that develops that deflects attention away from what is happening with your business, or the issue may burn itself out and never spread wider, but that will be taking a gamble. For effective issues management communication needs to be involved early, be offering strategic advice, and delivering tactical activity that moves towards a positive conclusion. The communicator's role in issue management starts before anything has happened and concludes when the response is evaluated. There are eight key roles that communicators should take in this process:

1 A communicator should provide an early warning of problems. They should be alert to the risks that the business has and also the areas where issues may emerge. Speedy identification and discussion of strategies to approach the issue within the business will help management of the situation and could prevent further escalation by allowing action to be taken.

2 Communicators can provide systems, or build on business processes, which will monitor for emerging issues. This should become a central strand of risk management and support the business processes. It is the PR and communication team who have the best understanding of, and ability to monitor, social media. Intelligence and information gathering is a critical function to support effective issue and incident management.

3 Communicators are problem solvers. They look at situations and develop responses, whether they are campaigns to promote a product, or staff engagement initiatives to connect with employees. This problem-solving approach is an important element when confronted with an issue or incident. They need to look at what is developing and work out the steps to intervene and reduce the impact on the reputation of the business.

4 Communication can and should be used as a way to intervene in a growing issue. This means the communicator must be ready to step in, and be trained, skilled and prepared to act. If this is in place they can move quickly with authority and develop appropriate plans.

5 Data and information that comes into the business should find its way to the communication team to support issues management.

The same information can support the day-to-day activities but becomes vital in the identification of issues and creation of responses. Action plans can be developed by taking account of feedback that the business is receiving. Any complaints should be carefully considered, particularly if they are unusual or unexpected. Customer services and frontline staff must be linked to communication to both inform the plans and help to disseminate essential information.

6 The communicator has a duty to speak 'truth to power'. Building strong relationships with executive teams will allow this to happen. It should always be done in a positive and supportive way as the aim is to put appropriate plans in place. This is not an opportunity to try to score points or build your own profile. It is a time to be honest and if the situation is potentially damaging, or the initial response from the business is poor or not working, this needs to be said. Once leaders are aware of the problems with the course of action being taken, they can review and amend activity or look to a new course of action.

7 Communicators are in a privileged position as they are able to bring into the business the views of those outside. This can inform the discussion. Bringing the views of stakeholders, shareholders, customers and others into the communication work should be the aim on a daily basis, not just when problems emerge. Communicators can use the data, information, tools and feedback on channels they are monitoring to develop a picture of what the issue looks like to people outside the business. This information is vital when considering the appropriate response to take.

8 Making connections across the organization is critical to the response and the communicator should bring key people together to map out the steps to be taken to manage an emerging issue. Remember that the issue or incident is unlikely to require the full response of the organization and all parts of it. So, it is important to know who has something to bring to the situation that can help in developing action plans. Know the people who matter and ensure they are ready to get involved to support the action plans.

CASE STUDY

What happened?

In September 2021, a video emerged of a woman who was coughing on shoppers at a store in Nebraska. The incident was filmed and placed on the social site Reddit by the person who had been affected by the actions.[6] It was reported in the *Independent* newspaper in the UK and *Newsweek* in the US, and happened at a time when Covid-19 restrictions were in place in the aftermath of the pandemic. The city of Lincoln where the incident took place had a directive requiring people over the age of two to cover their faces indoors. The woman said her allergies were the cause of the coughing, but she was also heard making disparaging comments about people adhering to the restrictions.[7]

The clip was also posted on Twitter, where it quickly gained more than four million views. As the woman was clearly shown in the footage she was swiftly identified, and media reports included details of who her employers were. Her details were easily found through her LinkedIn profile as the media worked to uncover her digital footprint.

The incident attracted significant media coverage and was particularly sensitive due to the many months of restrictions and regulations that people had been living under during the Covid-19 pandemic. Very quickly after the video footage went viral the woman's employers made a public statement that the incident had been reviewed and the individual no longer worked for them.

Throughout the media and social media activity the coughing woman said nothing and made no further comment.

What could have been done?

The situation can be looked at from a number of different perspectives. There is the view of the individual who filmed and circulated the footage, the view of the woman who coughed on the shopper, the view of the supermarket where the incident was filmed, and the view of the employers of the coughing woman. Each one has an opportunity to manage the situation and to protect their reputation by putting appropriate actions in place. It is important to take account of the circumstances and environmental factors that may affect how the situation is viewed. In this case coughing became anti-social or even criminal behaviour during the Covid-19 pandemic. It could potentially infect people and lead to serious illness or death.

The individual who circulated the footage had to consider the impact that their action would have, particularly as the woman was clearly identifiable.

In communicating with the media, they focused on the impact that the incident had upon them. There was no attempt to demand further action, a position which gave them some moral authority, appearing reasonable and with a community focus seeking to highlight what had taken place in order to protect others. This led to widespread coverage and support for the action.

In contrast, the woman who had coughed said nothing and gave no explanation of her actions. There was total silence about the situation. However, this has left questions unanswered, which will keep the incident at the forefront of the media's mind. Had she given an apology together with some understanding of why the outburst had taken place it could have been concluded. This could have been done by working with the media and being contrite.

For the supermarket where the incident took place, they were not called upon to make comment. They could have let the event happen with no comment and kept a distance from what happened. However, this is a risky approach as their actions and the way they work could be called into question and ultimately could lead to criticism. They should have been ready with an escalation procedure that would navigate the way forward if they were questioned or criticized.

Finally, the employers of the coughing woman had to step in quickly to demonstrate that her actions were not acceptable from a member of staff. It is a reminder of the importance of clear internal social media policies on how employees should operate on platforms. This will be covered in detail in Chapter 5. Having systems to monitor social media would have provided an earlier alert that an employee had been caught up in an incident. This would allow more time to identify what had happened, view the footage, speak to the employee, and consider the action to take. If the business, as in the case, takes decisive action quickly there can be a positive impact on their reputation. However, caution needs to be exercised; if there was any mistake in the understanding of what had happened, or if the employee was vulnerable or had dependants, the situation could quickly be seen as a heavy-handed response by an unsympathetic employer. Employers have a duty of care to employees, and this can create challenges in responding swiftly to issues and incidents. The business should consider the legal situation, the implications, and the public view of what has happened before identifying the course of action to take and the communication approach that is required.

KEY LEARNING POINTS

- Have monitoring systems in place to identify emerging issues.

- Ensure policies such as the use of social media are in place with staff.

- Develop escalation plans that can be used depending on how the issue develops.

- When under pressure consider working with the media to apologize and explain what has happened.

- Be clear that you have the full facts before acting or making public statements.

- As an employer be aware of your duty of care as assistance may be required.

- Take account of the circumstances and environmental factors surrounding the incident.

Conclusion

Dealing with issues and incidents can be challenging. If problems are allowed to grow, then within a short space of time they could be negatively affecting the reputation of the business. Effective management of these everyday problems requires plans to be put in place at the earliest opportunity. Spotting them as they emerge is essential. Communicators should be at the heart of this activity, ensuring they are able to provide intelligence and insight that the business can use. Knowing where these problems may emerge helps to prevent people looking for a needle in a haystack. The issue may get lost in a world of online and offline discussions, conversations, and content.

Understanding issues and incidents is assisted by considering how industries and professions that face significant risks put processes in place. Education, health and law enforcement professionals are more exposed to issues so have structures that support them. Their definition of what makes an issue or critical incident can help others to focus on what matters most. While issues can emerge from any aspect of the business and what it does, there are six aspects to focus on: people, product, policies, perceptions, finances, and environment. Remembering these six aspects can support learning and development towards better issues management. If people are struggling to know where to start to manage issues, they can look first to these areas to consider what is happening and how it may develop. Systems and procedures can help with this but so too can having an inquiring mindset. Communicators need to avoid becoming complacent in the work they do and remain alert to the problems that may develop and become issues.

Issues and incidents share many similarities. However, incidents usually have a physical element that has taken place while issues are based in perceptions. Both need to be addressed, as if they remain unchecked they will continue to grow, damaging the business, its reputation, and ultimately its profitability. Issues that grow can become crises that threaten the very existence of the business. Early identification and intervention remain the most effective way of starting to manage the situation. It is at this stage that the circuit that develops to create the issue can be disrupted or broken to limit the development and impact. There is no inevitability that a problem will grow to become a serious issue for the business. The right action at the right time and in the right place can manage the situation and allow plans to be implemented that bring it to a satisfactory conclusion. The way to do this is to put communication at the heart of the business, the developments, the discussions, and the response. Communicators have a key role to play and need to have the appropriate training that allows them, with support, to step in and manage both issues and incidents. They also require the right structures and framework to allow them to develop interventions that can manage the issue, and this is what we will look at in the next chapter.

Notes

1 Cambridge Dictionary Online, Meaning of butterfly effect, www.dictionary.cambridge.org/dictionary/english/butterfly-effect (archived at https://perma.cc/WM7X-MTB6)

2 Cambridge Dictionary Online, Meaning of issue, www.dictionary.cambridge.org/dictionary/english/issue (archived at https://perma.cc/5TEA-BRD4)

3 Birmingham Resilience Team (2019) Critical Incident Management for Schools, www.birmingham.gov.uk/downloads/file/1405/critical_incident_management_guidance_for_ (archived at https://perma.cc/QVK6-U8PS)]

4 NHS online (nd) Incidents, www.england.nhs.uk/contact-us/privacy-notice/how-we-use-your-information/safety-and-quality/incidents/ (archived at https://perma.cc/EF8U-AWNY)

5 College of Policing (nd) Introduction and types of critical incidents, www.app.college.police.uk/app-content/critical-incident-management/types-of-critical-incident/#background (archived at https://perma.cc/C97K-HMLU)

6 Kilander, G (2021) Woman loses job after being filmed coughing on people at Nebraska grocery store, *Independent*, 12 September, www.independent.co.uk/news/world/americas/nebraska-woman-cough-grocery-covid-b1918756.html (archived at https://perma.cc/2DTH-A3DE)

7 Palmer, E (2021) Janene Hoskovec, woman filmed coughing on shoppers in Nebraska grocery store, fired by SAP, *US Newsweek*, 09 September, www.newsweek.com/maskless-woman-coughing-nebraska-fired-sap-covid-19-virus-mask-1627321 (archived at https://perma.cc/UN2R-ERPN)

2

Creating the structure for issues response

Introduction

Developing an effective response to problems and issues requires the ability to bring together key people with relevant skills. Communication alone cannot successfully halt the progression of a problem and departments across the business need to be involved. But the PR and communication team can, and should, play a key role in the identification of emerging issues and in developing the plans for the way forward. Communication should have a wide span of oversight and the ability to deep dive into potential problem areas within the business. Issues and incidents that develop will rarely touch all parts of the business because if that situation occurs you may already be facing a crisis.

Problems when they emerge will affect particular parts of the business and it is these sections that will need to be involved in determining the solution. But issues and problems will always involve communication and senior managers or leaders within the business. This creates challenges in developing a structure or framework for issues response that will work across the whole organization. It also presents a challenge to ensure that everyone within the business understands how things work, the role that they will be required to play, and the fundamental principles underpinning the response. This can be overcome by creating a clear understanding of issue and incident management across the business and of how the responses will be developed, managed and coordinated.

This chapter will consider the governance processes and structure that can support issues management. It also details the focus that needs to be brought to day-to-day communication development and implementation.

Establishing governance procedures

Governance is usually considered in relation to the way the business decisions are made, managed, and monitored.[1] It is what ensures that risks are being managed, plans are being made in a strategic way, and performance is being monitored. At the heart it explains what will be done and by whom, and how it is reviewed and evaluated. Good governance is a key part of operating a successful business and within this structure issues management should also be included. Organizations often rely on having a crisis management structure that will allow them to operate effectively when looking at managing issues and incidents. However, this is not always the case. Crisis structures can be too unwieldy and narrowly focused on the most serious situations, which makes it difficult to adapt systems to address those day-to-day problems.

Crisis response focuses on mobilizing people across the whole business, whereas issues management will need to involve only relevant departments, as highlighted earlier. There needs to be a structure and system that will support the effective management of everyday issues. Reporting lines need to be clearly outlined, particularly where they may involve a change to existing day-to-day structures. This is particularly important when seeking a swift resolution to an emerging problem. An organization can only move quickly when it has relevant plans in place. Alongside this, the way information is shared, and by whom, is an important part of the framework for issues management. The right people need to be involved without delay and need access to the right information. How this could operate will be discussed later in this chapter.

Why have a structured response?

Having a structure in place to manage the response to emerging issues is essential for effective communication. If the business does not create an appropriate system to manage issues it can leave the communication team struggling to put a response in place, to agree actions and even to raise awareness of the growing problem. Communication needs to operate quickly to minimize any impact of an issue or prevent the development of a problem. For example, if there is a critical post on social media, the communication team needs to have the authority to make an initial response to attempt to diffuse the situation. Or if there has been an ongoing problem with a new service or product, the communication team can monitor and respond to individuals to address their concerns.

Delegated authority needs to be agreed and discussed as part of the planning and preparation of managing issues and incidents. When planning for issues management, communicators should ensure discussions have taken place with senior managers about the processes and messaging. This can ensure agreements are in place that give the communicator the flexibility to act without constantly seeking approval. Agreeing the parameters of this will give the communicator freedom to step in and attempt to mitigate the situations or put measures in place to resolve the issue. In many cases listening to the people raising concerns or experiencing the issue and offering to find a way to resolve it can achieve early resolution to the situation. This early resolution prevents the problem growing and developing further, which ultimately will protect the brand, business, or organization from reputational damage.

Negative comments, situations and events can swiftly become a reputational crisis if allowed to grow, develop, and mature unchecked with no intervention. Communicators are the one group of employees that hold the organization's reputation in their hands. When they put strategies and plans in place, they have the ability to show the organization at its best and increase people's confidence in it. A good reputation is important to the stability of brands and organizations; in Chapter 3 the issue of reputation management will be discussed in more detail.

Connecting the response

Building the response around a framework that has been agreed within the business will limit the chances for a slow response, for the issue to grow and develop, for confusion about what actions are being completed by whom, and for failure to respond. A communication structure for the response to issues cannot operate in isolation and needs to be part of the wider business structure. This connectivity is essential to the interventions that are made, as communication and the operational business need to work together to be effective. Communication alone may have the desired outcome, but more impact can be made when the response plan brings both together. Practically, this requires key departments to agree on the structure that is created and to understand their role in issue and incident management.

All of this work must be considered, agreed, and put in place to improve the approach to dealing with problems that affect the business. If there is a reluctance for certain sections of the business to devote time and energy to putting this in place, then use examples of where ineffective and uncoordinated issues management has had a significant impact on a brand, business, or organization. Some examples feature in the case studies within this book. Assessing the health of the brand, confidence in the business and the reputation of the organization can demonstrate where problems have grown to become issues and possibly even crises. When leaders and managers within the business can quantify the impact poor issues management can have on the bottom line, they may be encouraged to raise it up within their priorities.

Types of structure

In designing a structure that will work for a business it is important to understand the existing structures, roles and responsibilities within the communication team and resources that are available. Every member of the communication team needs to be able and willing to be involved in issues management. There is no place for people to shy away from recognizing when problems are emerging and developing response plans to put in place to address them. Issues and incidents do not always happen neatly during office hours or the working week. Many will happen, or start to appear, at night or at the weekend or during holiday periods. This means that everyone within the communication team needs to be able to move quickly to consider challenging situations and to develop interventions. Some organizations may outsource their issues management to specialists and PR agencies. In such situations the in-house team still need to understand the principles, responses and interventions required to manage situations. The external support should bring a level of knowledge and experience that boosts the team and helps to build skills. Even if the in-house PR resource is not going to directly manage issues, they will have a key role to play in the identification phase, as well as working to maintain confidence in the brand or organization.

Training in issues management is important and should be part of the professional development of all communicators. It does not matter whether they are working in media relations, digital developments, internal communication, or any other aspect of communication, they all have a part to play in effectively managing issues and incidents. Everyone needs a basic level of knowledge about how to approach issues management and to understand how it impacts on their work. Beyond the communication team, training needs to be in place across the organization to increase the ability of key employees and teams to move quickly to respond. This training can also increase opportunities to identify issues at an early stage, as a range of employees will be monitoring for emerging situations across the business. Developing a structure to manage issues will give employees a focus on ways they can get involved. It is essential that whatever framework is in place, it works for the business, existing meeting structures, and can break through any hierarchy. If there are too many layers of bureaucracy it can delay agreements being made to act, or even prevent identification of emerging problems in the first place.

There are five communication structures that can be introduced to address issues and incidents:

1 Outsourced team

2 Internal team

3 Quick response team

4 Joint response team

5 Issue response approach

With each of these structures there are benefits and challenges, which is why they need to be evaluated within the existing operation of the business. One size will not fit for every organization and factors including risk management, resources, brand identity, geographic location, history, and customer service need to be considered. There may be other elements to take into consideration based on the way the business is structured such as shareholders, stakeholders, and market dominance. Be clear about what the business wants to achieve in managing issues as this will impact on the structure that is put in place.

Outsourced team

In this situation an external PR agency or specialist issues management agency is brought into the business to deal with problems. This will help to boost a small communication team and provide knowledge and experience to manage issues more effectively. Finding the right agency to support the business will be critical, as will putting structures in place to provide clarity about when and how they will be required to step in. But this will only work if there is budget in place to pay for this additional support. It also works better in organizations that are not carrying significant risks. With many risks comes the requirement to step in to deal with more issues, which under this model would require more work and therefore lead to an increased cost. There is also a challenge for the specialists being brought in as they have to understand how the business they are supporting operates. If they fail to understand the DNA of the business, there will be an impact on their ability to respond.

Internal team

Larger organizations can have a dedicated team working on managing problems, issues and incidents. This may involve those working in business continuity and emergency planning functions. Such a team will have significant expertise in how to respond to low-level issues, putting mitigation in place to limit the impact and ensure that it does not become a crisis. The team should be alerted quickly to any emerging issues so that they can take control, develop action plans, and monitor any developments. To deal with growing issues, additional staff may be seconded into the team for the duration of the management of the situation. This structure will build knowledge and expertise but within a small group of employees. In turn this may lead others to step back from any responsibility for identifying and responding to issues and incidents.

Quick response team

This structure will bring together a team to respond to emerging problems and issues. They will be taken from existing roles to come together, allowing attention to be focused on intervening and monitoring the impact of actions. Those involved will have skills and experience in the subject that is emerging, in the actions that are taken, and, of course, communication. The team may work solely on the issue for a period of time, and then return to the day job but may be recalled or reconvened as required. For example, if there are complaints about a product the team would involve someone from the manufacturing team, from the distribution team, from management, from the logistics team who will have sourced materials for the product, and from the communication team. Those who may be brought in as part of the response team need to have received training or be experienced in incident management and response. This will allow them to come together quickly and to start to act.

Joint response team

In this situation an organization or business will work with others from outside to tackle the issue or will work with other businesses within the group. This can be seen in multinationals and businesses that have a diverse portfolio. Individuals with experience and knowledge can be brought together to address the situation, and consider mitigation and action that is required across the organizations. In public bodies this can be seen when identifying an issue that may affect the public receiving services from a number of organizations. For example, rumours may circulate on social media that a particular location is becoming a 'no-go area'; a joint response would bring together the local authority, police, emergency services and health providers to develop interventions.

Issue response

In some organizations there is a very informal structure that means people work on problems on an issue-by-issue basis. This may be due to the size of the business or infrequent issues and incidents occurring that need to be managed. When an issue is identified, it has to be highlighted to management before interventions are considered and discussed. The action may be taken in isolation, or after consultation with other key individuals. For some businesses this is an approach taken in the initial stages and a team will be brought together only if the issue develops and becomes more challenging. For example, a negative social media post about the business may be replied to by the social media or communication team. However, if this situation develops with further criticism, tagging the media into posts, or creating a campaign against the business then a team will be brought in to plan the way forward.

Whatever structure you use within the business it needs to be one that is flexible to the changing situation and responsive so that quick action can be taken when needed. In businesses that are reluctant to create a structure to work across departments the communication team would still benefit from putting in place a framework to support their issue and incident response. This will assist the everyday communication activity by recognizing problems that need to be escalated and having a clear process to do it. A significant amount of information is gathered by and passes through the communication team on a daily basis. In many cases action can be taken by the team without the need to involve others but when this is not enough the communication team need to spot it and take alternative action. A starting point will be to make others aware of the emerging problem and to consider a range of interventions. But critical to the issues management process is being able to identify and be alert to problems.

IN FOCUS

The Education Authority (EA) in Northern Ireland[2] has a Regional Critical Incident Response Team (CIRT) that has clear processes and procedures to deal with critical incidents that may emerge in the more than 1,200 schools and youth service provisions across Northern Ireland. The Department of Education in Northern Ireland (DE) defines a critical incident as: 'any sudden and unexpected incident or sequence of events which cause trauma within a school community, and which overwhelms the normal coping mechanisms of that school.' Each school is recommended to have their own critical incident policy, management plan policy and critical incident team to assist them in being prepared for and responding to a critical incident. All schools and youth service provisions can contact the EA CIRT, who will provide critical incident management advice and support as well as psychological first aid for pupils and staff as required. The EA CIRT operates during and out of office hours to ensure that schools and youth provisions receive timely critical incident support.

The role of the EA CIRT is to enhance the school's pastoral care system by providing critical incident management advice, support and resources to allow the school staff to successfully manage a critical incident. It is managed by a Regional Head of Service who is supported by a small core staff team and relies on staff who volunteer from a range of cross-directorate disciplines and services within the Education Authority. This multi-disciplinary team includes staff from a range of services including the EA's communications team who provide communications support as required to help schools to deal with media enquiries and to develop media statements.

> All members of the EA CIRT receive four days of induction training and are provided with a CIRT handbook of resources and relevant documentation. The EA CIRT meets on a termly basis for staff development and training.[3]

Communication briefing system

Every day, huge amounts of information will be in front of the communication and PR team. There will be questions from the media, alerts on social media, feedback from customer service teams, updates on existing activities, and the development of PR campaigns. Being able to identify those critical and emerging issues from that mountain of information is as challenging as finding a needle in a haystack. Developing briefing and information structures can support this work, alongside training that will help to develop the team. In addition, the systems will provide a simple way to raise awareness of issues and the management of them within the organization. The structures provide ways that information will flow into the communication team and then around the business. At the heart of it there should be regular touchpoints, which may be meetings or briefings, where information can be discussed.

Information comes into the communication team from many places. It may be from external or internal sources; it may be from monitoring social media or the mainstream media; it may be from business data and analytics or from anecdotal information. What matters is that the communication team are open to receiving all this information and insight, and then identifying what it may mean as well as what happens with it. There may be a chance to refine and develop communication strategies, to identify a PR campaign that may be required, or to implement some internal communication on the back of the insight that has been gathered. Activities should also be informed by what happens in the world around the business, the data inside the business and information, and learning from previous communication and PR work. Effective communication cannot exist in a bubble. The communication team must have regular meetings with senior managers to look at learning from previous activities, current and future actions, as well as emerging issues. Including those emerging issues will be vital to effectively monitoring and responding to problems before they grow.

Within the team each person has the potential to come face-to-face with an emerging issue and needs to be ready to alert colleagues and managers to what is happening. This can be helped by regular team catch-up sessions once or twice a day depending on the level of risk and issues that an organization faces. At the start of the day there is an opportunity to highlight an area of concern to colleagues so that more information may be gathered and if necessary immediate interventions can be agreed. With larger teams and those managing significant risks a further quick meeting later in the day can set the communication agenda for the rest of the day and plan for the following day. A team member will explain what has happened, what detail they have on the situation, and what they have done as part of the initial intervention. Colleagues can then consider if there is additional information they have to assist, provide an update on issues that may impact on the situation, and define the actions that are required.

The daily meetings should be supplemented by weekly reviews and monthly meetings. Weekly reviews will assess the problems and the actions that have been taken. They will consider what additional actions may be required and keep the situations in check. Close management of issues may be required if they take place over a protracted amount of time. Monthly meetings can look at trends, developments, emerging issues, and risks that may be appearing. This information can then support the organizational risk management processes as well as supporting the immediate response. Today's problems and issues can become tomorrow's risks and crises for an organization. This is where the issues management process should support and inform the risk management as well as the crisis communication planning. Although the two are separate, there is an interconnectivity between them that, when developed, can improve both incident management and effective crisis communication. An example of a risk communication structure is shown in Figure 2.1, which includes the links between the meetings.

FIGURE 2.1   Example of a risk management communication briefing structure

```
                    ┌─────────────────┐
                    │ Organizational  │
                    │  risk meeting   │
                    └─────────────────┘
                             │
┌─────────────┐    ┌─────────────────┐    ┌─────────────┐
│             │    │ Monthly comms   │    │             │
│ Risk matrix │────│ risk management │────│   Ad hoc    │
│             │    │    meeting      │    │ developments│
└─────────────┘    └─────────────────┘    └─────────────┘
                             │
                    ┌─────────────────┐
                    │ Weekly updates  │
                    └─────────────────┘
                             │
                    ┌─────────────────┐
                    │ Daily review in │
                    │    high-risk    │
                    │    moments      │
                    └─────────────────┘
```

With the implementation of a briefing system there is an opportunity to gather information about those regular issues and incidents that happen more frequently. A huge amount of information will be considered over time, and it should not be ignored as it can assist with communication planning. Once the details have been collated over a period of some months or up to a year it can allow the communicator to document the escalation plan for such problems. An escalation plan documents what actions should be considered or taken at each stage as the situation develops. This can be informed by events and will assist the communication team in managing issues. The system is a way to keep issues in check but also to become more effective at the ongoing management of situations that risk becoming negative and impacting on the business. But a system will only be as good as the data and information that is put into it, so getting relevant news and points to include is critical.

Finding the information

Within all the information, data and insight that reaches the communication team there are those problems and the start of emerging issues and incidents. Being able to identify them is a skill that some have, and others can develop. At the heart of this identification process is listening to what happens both within the organization and outside it. It is being aware of the developments that are taking place within the organization and considering what problems may follow from them. In some situations, this may help the business to look at how plans are developed and implemented to prevent problems before they happen, or they may just remain aware of the concerns that have been raised. Recognize the developments that take place in the world internationally, nationally, and locally. Any one of these developments may have an impact on the business and lead to issues and challenges. For example, if there is a problem with the manufacture of a rival's product it will put a spotlight on the business and any small issues may be quickly magnified. In short, the start of effective issues management is about having an alert and aware communication team.

Gathering information and intelligence should happen across a wide range of sources. Close to the communication team is the monitoring of social media platforms and gathering intelligence and information from media relationships. Intelligence gathering means that every time the media make contact about a problem or area of concern requiring a response it is an alert to an emerging issue. Every time media statements are developed, they are an opportunity to limit the impact of an issue or incident. Using a database or system to log the details of media queries and the response that is given is essential to effective issues management with the communication team. This will be covered in detail in Chapter 5.

Check your sources

As well as social media and the media, information will be available from employees and internal communication processes and activities.

This may be through existing formal channels for feedback but also may be through informal conversations and the organization's 'grapevine'. In some situations, the office gossip may be the first alert to an emerging issue within the business. On becoming aware of the situation, it will be important to cross-check with other sources to assess the reality of the subject under consideration. It is possible that someone may be unhappy about a development within the business, but their understanding of the situation is wrong, or they have misinterpreted it. Being alert does not mean taking at face value everything that is highlighted or presented as a problem. The provenance of information should always be considered when reviewing it and looking at potential next steps.

Stakeholders can also highlight information, particularly if they are involved in the monitoring and assessment of aspects of the business. Stakeholders bring insight from being aware of the way the organization operates but also from having an independent view of situations. They can also assist in the response to issues by offering support, advice, or third-party endorsement. However, there needs to be caution involved, as the relationship can become strained by the issue under consideration. As with all information it needs to be carefully considered and assessed before the next steps and possible interventions are developed. Shareholders may also provide valuable information, but they may be unnecessarily focused on the emergence of a problem or issue. This concern and nervousness can become an issue in itself, so again shareholders must be a key audience and linked to the flow of information. There are other potential sources of information from customers which may come direct through social media or indirect through customer services teams. Businesses that are involved in the supply of goods or services to support the operation are also important to the information flow.

An issue or problem that they face may become an issue or a problem that the business has to face. It is part of the external environmental factors that communicators need to be alert to. Being aware of conversations and developments around the business and within it is fundamental to effective issues management. It helps the understanding of where problems are and where they may be in the future. Be alert to situations, to developments, to comments and to changes that may impact on the business, its staff, and the way it operates.

TOP TIP

Put a logging system in place where details of issues, incidents and media enquiries can all be captured. Having oversight of the information will assist in being alert and monitoring emerging situations.

Where communication sits in the business

Communication is about more than just promoting products and services or attempting to protect the reputation of the business. It is an essential part of the way any organization or business is run and should operate as a central function and trusted adviser. This means working outside what may be seen as the traditional boundaries of communication. It is when stepping outside the boundaries that the work to manage issues and incidents becomes more effective. Communication has a lot to offer the incident response beyond just deciding what to post on social media, say to journalists or highlight to staff. The starting point is being part of discussions about the business development and also the risks that may be faced. Getting involved in the way the business secures its position and is looking to grow or restructure is important. It is about more than looking for a seat at the top table. Being a strategic adviser is important but more important is being recognized as someone who understands the way the business operates and has something to offer. Gaining credibility and confidence from within the business will assist when discussing and developing plans and approaches to tackle issues. Similarly, an understanding of the risks is critical to the development of communication. It provides valuable insight into areas to be aware of, as well as seeing how the business will identify and manage issues.

Confidence in communication cannot be built by one method alone; it takes time, care, and attention to achieve the required result. Connecting with key departments and individuals within the organization is a starting point. Find out what they do, how they operate and where issues are identified and managed. This can also help them to understand what communication can do and how it supports the business. The more people can see how communication works as an arm of the operational response to managing problems, building activities, and dealing with crises, the easier it will be when a situation emerges. Briefings will support the early alert to any situation or issue and people will recognize when to involve communication, as well as how to highlight situations to communicators. The early discussion of a problem can make the difference in the effective management of it. Organizations with a culture of blame will be a huge challenge to communicators. In these businesses any issues, problems, or moments when something is seen to have gone wrong will be covered up with an attempt to hide them from view – of those outside the business but also those within it. In doing this the ability to intervene and manage the situation is minimized and at worst lost. Creating a culture that is open and recognizes the learning opportunities presented by problems is important for all organizations.

Getting connected quickly

In the management of issues, the communication team should be among the first to be alerted to any problems. With many situations emerging initially on social media or through the news media, the communication team will often be the source of information about what is happening. Where the issue does not arrive from media, social media and communication, it is important the communicators are brought in as soon as possible to be aware of the situation and consider the options for managing it. The hard work of getting connected with departments and teams across the business will pay dividends when a problem occurs. Other teams will be aware of what communication can do to support the response and will alert the communication team at an early stage. Intervention needs to be considered swiftly but it is vital to avoid rushing to act. Consider the situation and consequences fully before assessing the options. It may be beneficial to consider developing incident and issues management training to upskill the workforce. This can include explaining the structure that is in place to respond as well as the role of communication and others. Explaining how the media and social media operate with regard to issues management would be central to this training, together with a discussion about the interventions that can be put in place. Employees need to understand the importance of effective issues management to the health of the business and its reputation. This work can also be supported by media training that will equip people to speak about issues and incidents. Anyone at a senior level in a business should be comfortable undertaking media interviews and at short notice. Giving them the skills and the techniques that are required should be part of their professional development.

Working to manage stakeholders and map issues is central to the systems operated by the communication team. Stakeholder management is essential to all forms of day-to-day communication and PR activities, but when managing issues it becomes critical to have networks in place and be able to connect with them at a moment's notice. Stakeholder mapping will identify those organizations and individuals that are critical to the business and who need to understand what is happening and developing. They are the people and organizations who can provide third-party endorsements, or they may intensify pressure by demanding more information and answers. If they publicly challenge the business, whether it is through news media, social media or some other way, it can have a significant impact. Communicators need to understand who these groups are, where they are, and what issues they are particularly interested in. This will assist when interventions are being developed as they may involve these stakeholders. For example, if you have an employee who has been behaving inappropriately on social media and it has been brought to the attention of the business, and you have an advisory group or shareholder that is vocal about online issues and bullying, then they will be key to consider when developing the response. If you forget them they may be publicly asking questions, which can impact on confidence in your response. But if you involve them by providing information about the situation and what is being done, and provide updates, they can become a powerful ally.

Use issues mapping to develop an understanding of the risks that may be faced by the business and the impact they can have on the reputation of the business. In unpicking those large risks you can identify vital information on day-to-day problems. Mapping those concerns, where they connect and how they can escalate will make it easier to spot where and how interventions can be made. Ahead of a problem emerging, understanding the risks will also assist in the mitigation of the issue by directing activity that can support effective reputation management. For example, if there is a risk of online negativity linked to a product or service, then you can map the issues involved. These may be a lack of understanding about the product, dislike of a change in the product, poor online reputation, or lack of responsiveness on social media. Breaking down these issues makes it easier to see the actions to take. This issues mapping can be undertaken on a regular basis to support the issues management processes and the mitigation of organizational risks.

The shape of communication

It does not matter if the communication team is one or two people or up to 100, being able to manage issues and incidents is something everyone can and should do. As a communication professional you need to understand what contribution you can make to managing problems and issues on a daily basis. If you are a strategic communicator working at a senior level managing a team, then you need to be setting the structures in place, supporting staff with training on issues management, and advising the boardroom about emerging threats. As a media officer working with journalists, you can gather intelligence about the issues that are appearing and help with the understanding of the issues of the day. Each communication professional has a key part to play, regardless of their area of expertise.

Communicators have a unique perspective on the way the business operates and what it means for the work they do. This can be used to focus on improving the way issues are monitored, managed, and dealt with. A social media specialist can use data and insight to help map not just current issues but also emerging trends and threats. There is a huge amount of information that is contained within social media platforms and specifically by careful analysis of the business's social channels. Media officers can identify the links to key journalists and provide clarity about what their focus will be.

Listening to employees

In addition, those working in internal communication and employee engagement will have an ear to the ground about what is happening within the business. They will have intelligence and insight into the developments that may become problems for staff, or even reputational crises. This information will be vital to the day-to-day monitoring for emerging situations that may require intervention. A significant number of issues can come from within the workforce, including staff raising concerns about a change in the business, misconduct or inappropriate behaviour, business failures, or even a perceived cover-up. If there are people within the team working in public affairs, they will have a valuable contribution to make in stakeholder management and recognition of issues of concern from external factors. Anyone in forward planning will assist in monitoring and identifying those issues that may emerge in the future. Video and photographic skills can be maximized in creating visualizations to support the management of issues and bring interventions to life. No matter what the communication skill someone has, it has a role to play in the management of issues and incidents. This must be a whole team effort, with everyone playing their part in the identification and management of issues.

Marketing and advertising teams often work alongside but not within the communication team. This can impact on the response to an issue or incident as the two can become disconnected. The communication team will be focused on tackling the issue and working out interventions and long-term plans. The marketing team will be focused on promoting the business and its products and may be considering undertaking actions and activities that can impact on issue management. The two must work closely together to ensure no steps are taken within marketing that may impact on the issues management work that is under way. It is also important to remember that sometimes situations are created from the activities of marketing and advertising. For example, in 2017 Pepsi had to pull an advertisement that was felt to be trivializing the Black Lives Matter movement.[4] The advert was felt to be 'tone deaf' and sparked extensive criticism. This reminds us that issues management needs to involve marketing and advertising to minimize the risk of such situations occurring.

Anyone involved in issues management can bring their unique skills and experiences to the response. The key is investing in developing the skills that are needed for effective issues management. This is more than just having communication skills if you really want to make a difference. Some of the key skills that are required include:

- news awareness
- investigation skills
- business knowledge
- analytical decision making
- empathy
- acting ethically
- influencing
- collaboration
- awareness of psychology
- resilience

News awareness

People need to have a 'nose for news' and understand what the media will be looking for in a story. This includes what makes a problem become newsworthy and how you can use this to recognize the issues that matter to the business. It requires an understanding of the news agenda that exists at the time. News agendas can change depending on circumstances and environmental factors, with some issues being raised up the agenda because of wider issues.

Investigation skills

Being effective in managing issues requires a detailed and methodical consideration of the factors involved. It requires the communicator to become a detective, gathering all the relevant information to ensure effective decision making and planning. It means asking questions and ensuring no aspect of the issue is ignored.

Business knowledge

All communicators need to have a good understanding of how the business operates, what matters to the bottom line, how the money gets spent, and what the priorities are. It includes having knowledge of the risk register and the risk management processes, understanding how trends and problems are identified, and how implementation of plans occurs.

Analytical decision making

Making effective decisions, particularly when under pressure, is a significant challenge. It is essential that communicators understand and can work with the data and analytics that are available, whether they are from communication activity or business insights. Being able to review them will increase understanding about the issues, which can then be assessed before decisions are made. The issue of effective decision making will be covered in Chapter 7.

Empathy

It is not just about using the facts and figures; the impact on people is a critical factor in identifying and managing issues and incidents.

Communicators need to understand how people are affected and how they feel. This requires actively seeking key groups out and then ensuring extensive listening takes place. Issues will always be more effectively managed if there is a focus on helping and supporting people.

Acting ethically

Operating within a code of ethics is essential for communicators globally. This code is particularly pertinent when managing issues and incidents. It outlines standards that should be maintained to ensure there is no dishonest or inappropriate behaviour. Protecting the business and brand must not come at the expense of ethics.

Influencing

Being able to effectively influence both within and outside the organization is important. Within the business it can support the operation of a system to manage issues, while externally it can develop relationships that will assist in the management of issues and incidents. Communicators have to be able to explain the situation and the recommendations to intervene and manage what is happening and that requires the ability to persuade and influence positively.

Collaboration

Managing issues and incidents cannot be done by the communication team alone. Others need to be involved in the identification and interventions of problems that emerge. Being able to work effectively with others across the organization, with stakeholders, or even the public is critical. Working together can often bring better results as interventions will grow from considering all the angles.

Awareness of psychology

Understanding how people may think, feel and act is a critical factor for communicators. This is often part of behavioural communication, where people need to be encouraged to act in a particular way using communication. However, it can help in the planning for, and responding to, issues. There are many short courses in social psychology and behavioural science that can support communicators and help develop their knowledge.

Resilience

Being ready and able to continue to monitor and respond to problems can be exhausting. At times it can feel like pushing a boulder up a hill only for it to roll down and need to be pushed up another hill. Managing issues and incidents can be a rollercoaster. They will always affect businesses and that has to be accepted. Having an effective system to manage these situations can help to build resilience within the communication team, making it easier to handle events.

The first steps

When a problem has been identified there are some key first steps that need to be taken to ensure you are heading in the right direction. Start by ensuring that through the links you have across the organization, the communication function is one of the first to be aware of the emerging issue. Achieving this requires those involved in social media management to spot what may be an emerging problem. Instead of just replying to a comment, issue, or complaint they see on social media, they should consider what it may mean and ask searching questions. Posting an inappropriate response at an early stage can help a situation to escalate, so care must be taken. In addition, if there is anyone within the communication team or the business that has a forward-looking role then they are also at the frontline of issues management.

Once the communication team is aware of the developing situation the structure and systems can kick in to make sure that consideration of response is swift and likely to be effective. Before considering any interventions, the starting point is to really understand the situation, the issue and what it could mean to the business.

This means finding out what is known, what is unknown, and unpicking the details that people have about what has happened.

When developing an effective response to an everyday issue, the small things really do matter. It is why having a structure and systems already defined is so important. The policies and procedures cover the big things so that there can be a focus on the details of the issue. It is important to ensure that the situation is being looked at from a position of what is known now, but also what is known about the situation before it was identified. Use this to start to consider how it may develop in the future. Focusing on these elements can give a clearer picture and assist with scenario planning. The second step is to ask the six key questions: what, when, where, why, how and who. What has happened and what may happen? When did it happen and when will the situation change? Where did it happen? Why did it happen? How did it happen and how was it identified? Who is responsible for it happening? These are critical questions to run through to ensure that as much detail as possible is available at the earliest moment.

Communicators must understand who is involved in the issue. What do we know about them and how they may act if the situation escalates? If the situation has developed on social media, it is vital to understand the influence that they have and the impact that may follow linked to their online presence. For example, if there is an online complaint about the product or service then is the complainant well known? Are they well connected? Do they have a large number of followers? Are their followers active, which may lead to an escalation of the issue? Focusing on those who are affected by the issue at an early stage is essential for developing an effective response and building and developing it over time, particularly if more people become affected. This will be discussed in more detail in Chapter 6, which looks at the role of social media within issues management. Understanding the problem is the first step and helps to lay the foundations for an effective response by considering future scenarios. Having the right intervention at an early stage is part of the solution but we must also be ready to change, adapt and develop if the situation develops.

If there is clearly an issue developing, then others need to be alerted to the situation and, as outlined earlier, the structure will involve connecting with the right people for the issue under consideration. Have a mechanism by which you can practically get people together virtually or in person to agree the initial intervention. This may be through internal social media, contacting through telephones, or using messaging apps. Having this process already documented and in place will allow you to move quickly as action will be expected by the team and the business. The steps could be set out in an issue management plan that can be shared around the organization. The plan will include information about the structure that is in place, the key individuals and their contact details, initial steps to take including alerting those key people, gathering all the information, assessing the influence and impact those involved may have, and interventions for those key issues that have been mapped and risks that have been outlined. This will provide a simple guide to the initial steps to take to help those who have to take a lead in managing the response to an issue, particularly out of hours and at the weekend.

CASE STUDY

What happened?

On 15 August 2020, the Canadian Revenue Agency (CRA) and the Government of Canada Key Service (GCKey) reported a cyber breach.[5] Reports stated that people had started to contact them a week earlier saying there were attempts to log into individual accounts. The agencies had confidence in the system and did not respond quickly to the first messages that highlighted the issue. The organizations had not publicly responded to initial reports but had alerted the police on 11 August.[6] It was estimated more than 11,000 accounts had been hacked in an attack believed to have used stolen usernames and passwords. This is called 'credential stuffing', when details stolen in other previous attacks are used. The reporting once the issue became public highlighted problems with people being able to contact the agencies for advice, and also put the spotlight on the fact that some said issues had been reported back in May 2020.[7]

What could have been done?

The starting point is to have a framework in place that would have supported listening to customers of the services. The organizations should have been listening to their customers and as the first concerns were raised could then have started to review what was happening. After issues were being raised on social media, there was also a delay in any comment or response being made; this was unacceptable to concerned people. Once they were investigating the claims, they could have provided some reassurance to those concerned account holders. If this listening had happened some months earlier, then the situation may have been tackled at an earlier stage and would not have come to a head in August 2020. Cyber threats are a universal risk and threaten all businesses. This means work could have already been undertaken to outline an initial response plan and escalation procedures in the event of a cyber issue. Having plans ready to address such problems would mean a quicker response and the avoidance of delays. One of the first actions should have been to check who was impacted by the problem and who was raising the issues. Ensuring they knew what was happening and opening lines of communication would have helped to build trust and confidence. The organizations were open to criticism for involving the police but then waiting for a few more days before those affected became aware.

KEY LEARNING POINTS

- Prepare issue response plans for the biggest threats and risks to the organization.
- Ensure monitoring systems are in place to listen to customers and other commentators.
- Develop an issue management structure that allows swift responses to be made when required.
- Focus on the people who are affected and how you can intervene to bring a satisfactory conclusion.

Conclusion

There are issues and incidents that happen every day so it is easy to think that they are just part of the day-to-day work rather than something that should have a systematic approach. Creating an issue management framework supports an effective response. Developing a structure that works for the organization or business will assist in allowing a swift but carefully thought-through response. Use the framework and an issue management plan to focus on the situation and how to move forward. Communicators should aim to have a forensic understanding of the issue so they can look at what may happen, scenarios for the future, and how to map related issues. But this is not something that communicators should manage on their own. It needs to involve key people across the business and, if possible, the input of stakeholders.

Managing issues needs a range of skills to be in place. It is not enough for the communicator to just be excellent at what they do, they need to be equipped to do more. It means being able to act as a detective to unpick the situation, find out as much as they can, and look at where more information can be obtained. They need to see beyond the narrow focus of PR and communication to look at the business impact of the situation. Putting training and professional development sessions in place can help to bring the team and individuals up to date with what is required. Build the skills and test them in a controlled environment. This work can increase trust and confidence in the communication team and their ability to manage emerging situations with the potential to damage the reputation of the business. Communicators need to be comfortable with considering data and insight, and analysing the situation before outlining possible interventions.

All this starts with having the right systems and processes in place to provide support. Identify the issues that may need to receive more attention than others within a sea of information that hits the communication team every day. Spot the problem post within the vast amount of commentary on social media platforms and use media queries as a source of intelligence. Finding problems is not just for the communication team and so time needs to be invested in explaining the role of communication and what it can do to support others across the business. When employees know something is going awry, they need to know who to contact, and also know that there will be no blame. They must feel supported so that the issue can be effectively managed with minimum impact on the business and its operation. It is a question of ethics and the values of the organization, which is what we look at in Chapter 3. The role of reputation in the management of issues and how to introduce ethical decision making must underpin the interventions and plans that are made.

Notes

1 Chartered Governance Institute UK & Ireland (nd), What is Governance? www.cgi.org.uk/professional-development/discover-governance/looking-to-start-a-career-in-governance/what-is-governance (archived at https://perma.cc/SA76-PGHG)

2 Education Authority of Northern Ireland (nd), Managing a Critical Incident, www.eani.org.uk/school-management/in-an-emergency-school-information/managing-a-critical-incident (archived at https://perma.cc/UH66-KXGU)

3 Interview with Victoria Poole, Comms Manager EANI, 17 September 2021.

4 Victor, D (2017) Pepsi pulls ad accused of trivializing Black Lives Matter, New York Times, 5 April, www.nytimes.com/2017/04/05/business/kendall-jenner-pepsi-ad.html (archived at https://perma.cc/AG8A-S6G7)

5 Government of Canada website (nd), Cyber Incidents, www.canada.ca/en/revenue-agency/news/2020/09/cyber-incidents.html (archived at https://perma.cc/KD8M-RCSD)

6 Aiello, R (2020) CRA cyberattacks impacted four times as many accounts as previously believed, CTV News, 17 September, www.ctvnews.ca/politics/cra-cyberattacks-impacted-four-times-as-many-accounts-as-previously-believed-1.5109368 (archived at https://perma.cc/S9LY-EJMN)

7 Dunham, J (2020) CRA cyberattack victims say they notified agency about hack long before breaches confirmed, CTV News, 19 August, www.ctvnews.ca/politics/cra-cyberattacks-impacted-four-times-as-many-accounts-as-previously-believed-1.5109368 (archived at https://perma.cc/RT3M-VDMM)

3

Ethics, principles and reputation

Introduction

Reputation is defined by the *Cambridge English Dictionary* as 'the opinion that people in general have about someone or something, or how much respect or admiration someone or something receives, based on past behaviour and character.'[1] The key is to see that past behaviour and actions are going to form the foundation of how people view, or adjust their view of, the business or organization under consideration. It is also built on perceptions and views of the organization rather than facts and figures. This makes the work of communication fundamental to incident and issues response. What people think and understand about a brand or business and an issue that they may have had, or have read about, with that brand can be improved by an effective approach to the situation and to the communication surrounding it. Reputation does have a role to play when looking at managing issues, but should it be the primary focus of the communication activity that is undertaken? The starting point has to be understanding what you want to achieve by issues management, which is also important to the work that is undertaken to prepare for issues and incidents. This chapter will explore the role of reputation and how to ensure an ethical approach to issues management.

Is reputation the aim?

The aim of issues management should be to resolve the situation or bring it to a satisfactory conclusion for those involved, limiting the consequences of what has happened, and managing the implications of it. For the communicator this means working closely with those who can conclude the problem, while also identifying future impacts and scenarios, and explaining the situation in a way that will avoid negative views of the business. For example, if there is a complaint about a product the priority is to understand what was wrong with it and where the problem may have originated. Is this a one-off situation? Could there be a problem in manufacture, or packing, or distribution? What resolution does the complainant want? It may be that in taking up the complaint and offering a refund the issue can be neutralized so that those involved are satisfied with the result and the problem can then be addressed in the production. In this situation the reputation gets built from the actions that are taken to deal with the situation. No amount of telling people that there is no problem will bring about the same result, and will potentially escalate the issue. Words should support the actions that are taken. Building, managing or improving the reputation of the business or organization should come from these actions that are taken rather than be the sole aim of the activity.

If reputation management on its own is the aim in dealing with the problem, then actions will be taken to improve perceptions rather than address the issue. In the best case this can delay a situation becoming publicly known but in the worst case it will be seen as cynical manipulation of the circumstances. In the example of the product complaint, if protecting reputation is the focus and the situation in manufacture, packing or distribution is not rectified, then there will be further complaints. These can build and then escalate the situation so people become increasingly vocal, possibly angry and frustrated at what will be seen as attempts to keep them quiet about the problem. Communicators could find themselves ethically challenged if they are asked to make a problem like this go away without the business acknowledging the point being raised. Reputation should be a by-product of an effective issues management process, not the sole aim of the communication activity. In developing an incident or issues response plan it is important to clearly articulate the aim. In most cases, the aim should be the satisfactory conclusion of the situation with the minimum negative impact on those around it.

TOP TIP

When assessing a situation consider whose reputation should be, or is, involved. Is it the business, the customers, the staff, the stakeholders, the shareholders or others? Review the details of the issue and look at where it connects to people both inside the business and outside.

In reality an issue will affect all of these groups and so the perceptions each have of the situation should be a priority for the response plan. The degree to which each group is affected will vary depending on the circumstances of the problem that is being considered. This should be detailed within the response so the potential impact on the reputation of the business at the centre of the issue can be understood and appropriate actions included in the plans. The reputation of the staff may be brought into question if there is a fault or problem detected in the manufacture or provision of a service. The reputation of stakeholders may be called into question if the issue is linked or connected to them. The reputation of shareholders may be questioned if the problem appears to have been created due to some financial issue. And the reputation of the customers may be called into question if the problem is not as it seems and may be the subject of manipulation or misinformation. Understanding the implications of the problem might be overlooked as it is a small issue within the whole operation of the business. What matters though is being able to unpick the impact and implications so that appropriate action can be taken both operationally and within communication. This makes the development of interventions easier to identify as you work through the implications and then consider what steps may bring about a change. This will be discussed when looking at interventions to take in Chapter 4.

Operating ethically

Underpinning all PR and communication activity is the requirement to operate ethically. This is a vital element when considering the influence and impact that communication can and sometimes does have. Lacking ethics or ignoring the ethical implications of the work can lead communication into the realms of propaganda. There are many definitions of ethics within philosophy but put simply it is about a set of moral principles that deal with what is good and bad.[2] If we are operating ethically then it will be within an agreed set of principles of what is right and wrong. This matters, as within PR and communication there are agreed industry sets of principles for operation. These are set out by bodies such as the Chartered Institute of Public Relations (CIPR) and the Public Relations and Communications Association (PRCA) and govern what is seen as right and wrong for members to do in their day-to-day activities. Ethical behaviour in the workplace is the '... moral code that guides the behaviour of employees with respect to what is right and wrong in regard to conduct and decision making.'[3]

This makes it clear to see why the ethical framework for communication is important for the everyday problems and issues that are encountered. In the first instance it ensures there is no misconduct in the approach. For example, operating for the benefit of some individuals but not for the greater good, or even avoiding advising on action so that additional work is not created. Secondly, the ethical behaviour has an impact on decision making as in some situations communicators may personally benefit from advising a business to take a course of action. For example, suggesting a specific company is used to undertake some work, or to suggest undertaking a media interview because of personal connections. It is similar to sports professionals getting involved in betting scandals. They use inside information for personal benefit. Codes of ethics that exist include having to declare an interest when working with a particular client or business, and thus avoiding that ability to benefit from activities. With the scrutiny that exists of businesses and professionals from the media and the public, openly operating in an ethical manner is more important than ever before for organizations, businesses and brands.

Operating ethically needs to happen every day, whenever work is being undertaken, whenever advice is being given, and in developing plans and campaigns. It is not something to add into the end of the work processes but should be involved at every stage of considering, planning and implementing communication activity. In managing issues and incidents, communicators should ensure that frameworks, structures and plans that are in place to deal with situations are rooted in ethical decision making. Training for communicators on how to operate ethically and how to manage ethical dilemmas is important. It helps to set the tone of what is expected from the team and this is essential when they are called to respond to an emerging problem. Operating within a defined set of principles will support an effective intervention, and activity will withstand any scrutiny. In the aftermath of dealing with the situation, operating ethically will mean extracting the key learning in a non-partisan way. The most effective learning comes from having an open mind and a willingness to listen. Ethics may not be at the forefront of communicators' minds on a daily basis, but it should be ingrained in processes, procedures and decision making to ensure an effective response.

Why does ethics matter?

Ethics matters to the communication response to managing issues on four fronts: trust and confidence, reputation, responsibility, and decision making. Each element is a key part of the process to ensuring an ethical response to situations.

Trust and confidence

This is the foundation of all issues, incident and problem management. In reality it is fundamental to all aspects of communication.

Without it people would not use a business, would not buy certain products, would avoid specific services, and would not listen to the organization's messages. If there is no confidence that the product is good or that the service is the best it can be, then there will be a lack of trust in the brand or business. In these situations, the words will be at best meaningless and at worst seen as unethical, promoting a position that is not the reality. Focusing only on promotion can fail to take account of the reality that people face and the damage can be serious. The actions and the operation of the business have to match the words and images that are used. Credibility is key to building trust and confidence. Being a credible source of information is essential for an effective response to a problem.

Reputation

A brand or business that is seen to operate unethically faces a negative impact on its reputation. It may not happen immediately but as people become aware of the behaviour and the actions that have happened it will start to erode a good reputation. This can be seen with companies being accused of 'greenwashing', where they deceptively present information to persuade people of their environmental credentials. As people become aware, they are 'calling businesses out' for the deception and this causes damage to their reputation. Such situations can also have an impact on sales, profits and the viability of the business.

Responsibility

Failing to accept the situation and the organization's responsibilities in relation to it will damage reputation. This can happen in a number of ways including keeping quiet and hoping no one makes a connection with the situation and the business, putting others in the spotlight for your problem, or even 'gaslighting', where a business will make someone question their understanding of reality. In the worst cases this can clearly be seen as unethical behaviour as it manipulates understanding of the situation. Communicators need to be aware of this and actively avoid such situations. There is a responsibility in what they may say, what they do, and how problems develop.

Decision making

Ethical decision making has been the subject of discussion in virtually every profession. It is a critical element to an effective response to a situation regardless of what industry is involved and what issue is under consideration. Gathering information and making the best decision possible given the circumstances is important for all workplaces. But for the communicator it becomes even more critical as it means ensuring you look broadly at the situation in front of you, widen the scope if necessary, and avoid making decisions based purely on the business's requirements and protecting the reputation. Making effective decisions while under pressure and operating at speed to respond to a growing problem is challenging but processes and procedures can help. This will be covered in detail in Chapter 7.

Principles of ethical decision making

There are five key principles of ethical decision making in communication and issues management: independence, nonmaleficence, beneficence, justice, and fidelity. Each of these is essential when considering how to respond to an emerging problem or issue. Communicators need to be aware of them to support how they make judgements about a situation and decide on the action to take. Decision making is more effective when it takes a range of perspectives and views into account and is founded on taking the 'right steps' to bring about a resolution. The business may want to move quickly and demand a particular course of action, so this is when the principles can be used to ensure what is done is rooted in acting appropriately and with due care and attention to others:

- Independence is allowing people to make their own decisions and focusing on providing them with the best-quality information.

- Nonmaleficence is doing no harm to others, whether intentional or as an accepted indirect consequence.
- Beneficence is supporting people and being focused on doing good in managing the situation.
- Justice means treating people equally or being clear if this is not going to be the position.
- Fidelity is about an organization honouring its commitments, whether about a product or service.

In a situation where someone has complained about a product that does not work, the organization would need to accept its responsibility to have a product that works, be honest about what has happened, take no action to the detriment of the complainant, be clear what is going to happen, and allow the individual to take the information and make their own decision. The five points are critical to developing the interventions to manage a situation, minimize the impact, and prevent it escalating.

What are organizational values?

Values and ethics are not the same, although they are very closely connected. Values are the beliefs we have that guide our actions and behaviour, and our judgements of what is right and wrong. Ethics is a system of moral principles that people use to conduct their lives. Organizational values are the core principles and beliefs that underpin the operation of the business. It matters to ethical decision making because it is how the actions taken will be assessed and measured to judge if they are successful or not. A communicator can find themselves in a difficult situation if the organization's values require them to act in an unethical manner. It is why discussion about values within a business is important. This discussion allows them to be challenged, developed or refined, as necessary. In some cases, the principles of the communicator will put them at odds with the values of the business and this will cloud the ability to act and react to situations. It is important for the organization's values to work within the society in which it operates. If they don't, the organization will be perceived as being out of touch with life or with the communities in which it is working. For example, if a business is working internationally then the local customs, values and beliefs will need to be considered in developing plans, strategies and communication activity.

Discussions about ethics and values may feel like we are straying into a philosophical debate, but this is not the case. It is looking at the reality of people's perceptions, and perceptions are what matters when looking at the steps to take to deal with everyday issues and incidents. For example, if you are a fast-food restaurant that promotes that it is sustainable, but people are complaining about the packaging, it is important to consider the organization's values before deciding on a course of action to take. In this case the words are not seen to be matched by the actions of the business. There may be an accusation of 'green-washing' and pressure will be placed on the company to demonstrate clear ethical standards. All of these considerations are very practical and far from just a philosophical discussion.

The values of the organization are set by those at the top. Management demonstrate what is acceptable, supported and recognized as important to the way the business operates. They ultimately show what is valued in both their actions and behaviour. Praise, reward and recognition will go to those who embody the organizational values. If the values are not cognizant of ethics and public perception it will block an effective response to issues. Understanding the organization's values is important for communicators dealing with everyday issues and charged with developing appropriate plans. Failing to take note of the values has the potential to undermine any action that is taken to manage a developing situation. It means the action taken to address the issue may not be supporting what the organization stands for and this perceived conflict or disconnect can damage its reputation.

How can we damage an ethical response?

The challenge often comes from management within the organization failing to understand the implications of the actions that are being outlined. They may also lack knowledge of the role of communication and how it will operate when tackling a problem. The result can be communicators being told what to do without the opportunity to guide the conversation and to focus on what matters. If the management team become preoccupied with reputation and protecting the organization this will be problematic.

As discussed earlier, the action taken can only go so far to address any issues if it is prioritizing the business's reputation. Failing to take account of the other aspects of decision making together with a refusal to listen to the position of others will limit the scope of the response and the ability to make a positive impact. Management can also become focused on the personal impact that the issue may have on them. Those at the top of any organization or business have a lot to lose or gain from the management of issues. In the worst case they could see calls for them to resign as the problem moves into the realms of a crisis. It is this potentially negative situation that may be preoccupying their thoughts and impacting on their decision making.

In addition, the response can be challenged because the focus is on the financial loss or potential financial loss to the business, shareholders and others. This is a further way in which decision making and responses can be skewed to focus just on protecting the aspects that make money. It may make people unwilling to listen or recognize the wider impacts beyond the financial implications. Communicators can counteract this by finding ways to financially quantify the damage caused to the reputation if the issue develops or appropriate actions are not taken. It is important to remember that an ethical response requires wider consideration of the situation and its impact on people as well as the business.

A business that is not able to operate strategically, or where those at the top lack strategic oversight, will have a negative impact on the response to issues. The actions and focus will be on the immediate situation and issues and will fail to see the long-term implications. Decisions made for short-term gain may be detrimental to the future of the business. It is vital to see the future impact of the situation and in some responses a short-term negative hit to the business may be necessary in order to secure long-term viability.

Failing to understand or be interested in the detail of the problem that has emerged can also impact on having an ethical response. Understanding the detail of the situation is important to considering the issue at hand but also, crucially, to any escalation. It is in the detail that the potential future steps become clear and mitigation can then be considered. Trying to manage an emerging issue by just looking at what is in front of you can result in missing important detail that would refine the approach. Finally, the problem may just be seen as a 'PR issue' or even a 'PR disaster', which would put the responsibility solely with the PR and communication team while the operation of the business continues without being cognizant of what is happening.

In reality there are very few real PR disasters; they are usually challenges attributable to an organizational breakdown or business-related problem. They are just issues that require a PR or communication response. It is important to recognize that communication can take the initiative with issues management and lead the way in developing response plans. The key is to develop ways to address the elements that may lead to a poor or, in the worst case, unethical response.

Building the understanding of communication

There are four important ways that communicators can tackle a lack of understanding about the role communication should take in issues management. These elements must be built into day-to-day activities to build awareness before there is a requirement to respond to an emerging problem.

Talk about issues

Firstly, it is important to talk about issues management and the approaches that can be taken within the business and to do this before anything has happened. Opportunities will exist to demonstrate an alertness to issues when discussing developments within the business, changes, product and service amendments, and aspects of PR campaigns and initiatives. Showing an understanding of risk and risk management builds confidence in the PR and communication team. This work should be done consistently and over time demonstrates the breadth of thinking within the communication team.

Increase understanding

Secondly, it is important to raise understanding of the role that communication plays within issues and incident management. Some senior management may only call for communication advice in the event of a crisis, so it is critical to show that there are many opportunities to intervene and prevent or limit the impact of an issue, so it doesn't become a crisis. Those at the top of the organization may need their eyes opened to the direct impact that intervention by communication can have. This could be included in any training on PR, media and communication; systems can be discussed during staff inductions and promoted through internal communication channels. Remember that being able to give examples of what has happened, the action taken by the communication team, and the positive results it had will have a bigger impact.

Use case studies

Thirdly, maximize the use of case studies to highlight the approaches that are needed. Use case studies either from within the business or involving other businesses or organizations. Discuss issues management and look at what others have done, what worked and what could have been improved. Case studies also show the impact of issues and the management of them in the long term on a brand or business. This can be long-term damage to sales, brand position, reputation or the growth and development of the business. Highlight the ways in which communication can have a positive impact when involved from the early stages. Intervention and resolution of problems and issues can be brought to life through case studies.

Scenario planning

Finally, use opportunities for scenario planning, particularly in the development of projects or change programmes within the business. In these situations, a range of people from across the business will be involved, which broadens education about the role of communication in issues management. Looking at scenarios will then allow a discussion of the plans required and the escalation process for problems and issues. Escalation of activities will happen as the issue may develop, grow and build. The escalation plans are similar to a flow chart developed to document the approach that if X happens then Y will be the response; if XY then grows with Z then A will be introduced. For example, if there is a negative online review from one person with limited followers then the situation may be monitored. If in the monitoring another negative review is identified, then action would be taken with a response from the business to those complainants. Scenario planning is about looking at the 'what ifs' of situations.

TOP TIP

Develop a programme of training to equip both communication staff and those in key roles in the business with the skills to respond to incidents. Ensure this includes working through scenarios to consider how to ensure ethical decision making.

Defining the approach to take

Responding to an issue that has been highlighted needs to take a wide range of information into account. Careful consideration of all the information that is available will support effective decision making about the action to be taken. There is a seven-step system to assist communicators and ensure that they have clearly understood the emerging situation and can make decisions on the action to take:

1 Situational analysis – have a clear understanding of what the problem or issue is. This includes what the problem looks like and the span of the impact of it.

2 Scenarios – consider the ways the situation may develop both in the immediate and long-term future.

3 External factors – review the external factors and environment surrounding the situation and identify how it may impact on the situation that is emerging.

4 Values – understand the organizational values, culture and any aspects of the internal business operation that may be relevant to the situation and the response.

5 Third parties – consider the role of others and any impact on them from the situation. This means considering stakeholders, shareholders or even customers, what they will think and feel about the situation and what may they expect from any response. This is particularly important to consider if the problem or issue grows or is likely to escalate.

6 People impact – who will be affected by the situation that is developing and how could that impact spread to others? It is important to consider what the problem may mean to key people, whether they are customers or service users.

7 Understanding – consider what people know of the problem at this moment in time. Do they know about it and if not will it be very easy to spot as it potentially develops? Also consider if it is affecting a key area of the business, or if it could have an international dimension. Understand if the issue is a subject that people will be interested in. This can be linked to the level of interest in what the business does.

Working through those seven steps will ensure the communicator understands enough about the situation to be able to decide upon the approach that should be taken. It is important to recognize that reputation does not feature in that seven-step approach. There is a good reason that it doesn't, as it should not be the aim of the response, nor should it be the focus of the work that is undertaken. The aim of the issues management plan could be many things depending on the information that has been gathered in the seven-step system. It may simply be to conclude the problem and be able to draw a line under what has happened. For example, if there is a complaint about a product failure then it may be simple to respond and apologize, offer a replacement or a voucher, and then assess why the product did not work and what happened in production. This may then conclude the issue without the need to act further.

The initial aim may just be to understand the resolution that may be required to the situation that has emerged. If it isn't as simple as the example of the product failure, then the important step is to know what those involved in the situation require as a resolution. Ahead of the communication response, though, it is vital to know what the business response is. If there is no appropriate action being taken within the business, then no amount of communication will ensure an effective outcome to the issue. If the example of product failure develops and gets worse there will need to be some changes to the manufacture. The situation cannot just be ameliorated by communication activity. The communication should be brought in once the business has understood the product or service change that is required. If the impact then spreads and the issue grows then a more comprehensive communication plan will be required. There are many TV shows and media outlets that will investigate such problems and expect to see both business action and effective communication.

Taking an approach may involve wanting to challenge people's understanding of the business or industry. The issue or problem may be linked to a lack of awareness about how the business operates. Whether it is the manufacture or distribution you can use communication to shed some light on the way things work. The aim of issues management may be to build understanding of the business. Scientific industries, financial institutions and others may all struggle with issues being raised that are due to a lack of understanding about the business. In some situations, the issue cannot be simply dealt with so that it disappears. The best case would be to contain the problem to understand more about it, or to start work on remedial activities. Finally, the action is an opportunity to promote the organization's values as the situation develops. But care needs to be taken that this is not considered in isolation of the seven-step system.

CASE STUDY

What happened?

On Monday 22 March 2021, a post appeared on Twitter that alleged something that appeared to be shrimp tails had been found in a box of the cereal Cinnamon Toast Crunch in the United States. The man who posted the shocking discovery was Jensen Karp, a comedian. The story quickly became the talk of social media and in many respects it was because of the exchange that happened between @jensenkarp and @CTCsquares. The brand made a speedy apology, but this was followed with a change in their course of action. They claimed the discovery must be 'an accumulation of the cinnamon sugar'.[4] The situation then escalated when Jensen provided further information about finds in another box of the cereal that appeared to include dental floss.

  This became a very public feud with Jensen accusing the brand of trying to 'gaslight' him by their response.[5] A statement from the cereal manufacturers General Mills said: 'While we are still investigating this matter, we can say with confidence that this did not occur at our facility. We are waiting for the consumer to send us the package to investigate further. Any consumers who notice their cereal box or bag has been tampered with, such as the clear tape that was found in this case, should contact us…'[6]

  General Mills CEO Jeff Harmening told CNBC: 'Based on the information we have right now, it is highly unlikely this occurred at a General Mills facility. So right now, we're in the process of working with that consumer to try to figure out, kind of, what happened between when it left our docks and when he opened it.'[7] Tests were due to be carried out on the discovered items and the discussion ended but there were plenty of humorous memes and comments circulating.

What could have been done?

The social media team appeared to follow a standard plan to deal with a complaint made through social platforms. The issue started with a limited apology and the offer of a voucher to try and limit the impact and spread of the problem. This failed to take account of the full implications of the situation including the nature of what was found and the details of the customer. Using the seven-step system would have assisted in gaining a clearer picture of the situation that had occurred.

There was confusion about the real situation for the business. After the post by the manufacturer of the cereal said they had 'confidence' it had not happened at their facilities, it was qualified later by the CEO who dropped it to 'highly unlikely', casting some doubt on the initial claims. It appeared the business was responding too swiftly to try and distance themselves from what had happened. But the big turning point in this situation appears to have been when the Twitter account @CTCsquares suggested the items were possibly accumulated sugar. This led to the complaint that the brand was 'gaslighting'. This started to escalate the situation into a very damaging place where they appeared to cast doubt on the judgement and perception of the customer.

By taking some time to understand the situation and avoiding making swift commentary based on supposition rather than fact, the outcome may have been less volatile. The brand moved quickly, possibly in an attempt to protect their reputation from this emerging problem, but it denigrated the views of the customer. Having a clear plan that was focused on assessing the situation, appearing interested in the problem and trying to solve it, and working to be open and honest about the situation would have supported an improved response. Finally, the social media and customer services teams need to be connected to the PR and communication teams. This would have assisted in the understanding of the potential future problems linked to the response that was made. All communicators need to remember that each case is different and should be considered with an open mind. This will support the identification of key elements and factors important to consider in the response.

KEY LEARNING POINTS

- Recognize the potential of the situation and of the possible developments that may follow.

- Show that you care about the issue that has been raised and will be doing something about it.

- In a public discussion ensure that there is a way to show publicly that it has been concluded.

- Understand the way social media works and the need to respond quickly but accurately.

Conclusion

PR and communication are powerful forces within the management of issues and incidents, and need to be treated with care and operate within clear guidelines. This means the communicator needs to be aware of the impact that they can have, both positive and negative, on situations. Ensuring there is an ethical approach to the work is essential and PR and communication industry bodies have high-lighted what is required in codes of ethics. But ethics is not just for dealing with problems and issues; it needs to be part of everyday activities and discussions. Putting training in place that will encour-age communication staff to consider their actions and approaches within an ethical framework is good practice. It is through training and discussions that ethical plans and decision making can become the normal approach.

The primary aim of any issues management should not be to protect the reputation of the business. Focusing on this in isolation of all other factors will challenge ethics and potentially lead to a less effective response. Issues management is about much more than just communicating to protect reputation. But communicators need to know where they are and where they want to get to in dealing with the problem at hand. This is more than just addressing things through communication. Working across the business will bring about a more robust response. In making decisions about the response, ensure ethical considerations run right through. There is extensive scrutiny of businesses and individuals every day and any failure to live up to organizational values, or any attempt to use responses deemed 'greenwashing' or 'gaslighting' will be called out. The principles of ethical decision making help the communicator remain in the right place when developing plans to prepare for, and respond to, problems. All this matters to ensure that trust and confidence with the organization or business can be maintained.

Communication plays an important role in managing issues and incidents and this needs to be explained to the rest of the organization. Find ways to discuss incident response and the role of communication. It can be through training, using case studies and taking other opportunities when they arrive. Internal communication of issues management and the ethical approaches taken by communicators can build knowledge ready for when teams have to work together to respond to an emerging problem.

Systematic approaches to considering the problem from all angles will assist the understanding of where the business is and, more importantly, where it needs to be. This supports the development of plans including escalation plans and the consideration of scenarios that may follow. It is the same system that can help to support ethical decision making and ensure it is cognizant of organizational values. Reputation, ethics and values are all critical to building the trust and confidence that is required for effectively managing everyday issues. They are also essential when considering the interventions that need to take place, and this is what we move to consider in Chapter 4.

Notes

1 Cambridge English Dictionary online, meaning of reputation, https://dictionary. cambridge.org/dictionary/english/reputation (archived at https://perma.cc/ P7H4-XEA8)

2 Merriam-Webster Dictionary online, meaning of ethic, https://www.merriam-webster.com/dictionary/ethic?utm_campaign=sd&utm_medium=serp&utm_source=jsonld (archived at https://perma.cc/5M9W-42XJ)

3 Mahan, T (2019) How to define ethical behavior & why it's important in the workplace, Work Institute, www.workinstitute.com/how-to-define-ethical-behavior-why-its-important-in-the-workplace-2/ (archived at https://perma.cc/T45P-7NYW)

4 Marcus, E (2021) The curious case of the cinnamon toast crunch box, *New York Times*, 23 March, www.nytimes.com/2021/03/23/style/cinnamon-toast-crunch-shrimp.html (archived at https://perma.cc/9AXY-R623)

5 Venn, L (2021) What the hell is going on with Cinnamon Toast Crunch shrimp on Twitter, *The Tab*, www.thetab.com/uk/2021/03/24/what-the-hell-is-going-on-with-cinnamon-toast-crunch-shrimp-on-twitter-200158 (archived at https://perma.cc/NWF5-7AP2)

6 Meisenzahl, M (2021) General Mills CEO says it's 'highly unlikely' that any shrimp tails went into Cinnamon Toast Crunch at its facility, *Business Insider*, 24 March, www.businessinsider.com/cinnamon-toast-crunch-shrimp-tails-general-mills-ceo-refutes-claims-2021-3?r=US&IR=Tm (archived at https://perma.cc/D56P-3LVN)

7 Lucas, A (2021) General Mills CEO says company takes food safety very seriously after shrimp tails claims go viral, CNBC, 24 March, www.cnbc.com/2021/03/24/general-mills-ceo-company-takes-food-safety-seriously-after-shrimp-tail-claims-.html (archived at https://perma.cc/4LH3-7DSR)

4

Finding the right words

Introduction

The central 'golden thread' through the response to an issue or incident is the words that are used. Views, action that is taken, and approaches that are made have to be really clear to all who are listening, watching and taking notice of the situation. Whether it is referred to as the key messages, the values or the narrative, it is critical to document the position. This is more than what is said to the media or posted on social media. It is how you will sum up the situation and the business's response to it.

Communicators also need to be aware that words matter, and care must be taken in considering which words will be used. This requires a clear understanding of the situation and the views that exist around it. Understanding who is impacted by the issue is also a key requirement as it will assist message development. There is a note of caution that the communicator could use words that have the reverse of the intended effect. Instead of calming and easing the situation they can inflame it and make it worse. For example, statements may appear to undermine a point of view, or as in the case of the Cinnamon Toast Crunch case study in Chapter 3, may appear to be 'gaslighting' people. The aim is to appropriately respond to minimize the impact of the situation, to maintain trust and confidence, and limit damage to the reputation of the business. This cannot be done when the organization puts itself in a position of conflict. In addition, communicators need to be aware of cultural, geographic and other differences.

A word or phrase used in one country with one community may be acceptable but in a different country and circumstances would be inappropriate.

In creating the narrative or messaging it is essential to be listening both to what is happening and what is being said about the situation. This will provide indications of the mood and tone around the issue that is being considered. People may be angry, frustrated, annoyed, irritated, inconvenienced or just questioning about what is taking place. Words used to respond to the situation will change depending on what circumstances and views exist. Influencing the situation is only possible if you take account of the views that are in place. This chapter will explore how to define the words that are used, and the interventions that can be put in place.

Messaging matters

The words that are used to respond to a situation should help to paint a picture about what has happened and more importantly what is being done to address it. It is an opportunity to set out the key elements that the business wants to bring to the fore in discussion of the issue. The wording should seek to explain the issue and focus on actions that have been taken. It is that latter element that is the most critical as the response, when effective, can build confidence in the approach taken. Too much focus on explaining the issue will appear to be an attempt to minimize the significance of it. This can develop into a defensive position where the business seeks only to divert attention away from the issue and detract from what has happened. However, a successful outcome can be achieved with careful consideration of the wording used.

Wording should demonstrate the best of the business, brand or organization. It should embody its values and show how they are being supported by the response that is being taken. This may appear to put a huge emphasis on the words that are used but as will be explained in Chapter 5 when looking at the media, and Chapter 6 looking at the role of social media, it is the core of any response to an issue. The messaging that is used should be in place across all communication activity. It must be used by everyone responding to the issue no matter what they are doing – this will ensure consistency. Depending on whether it is in internal messaging, a media statement or a post on social media the words may be slightly different, but they should support the same narrative or key message.

There is a decision to make as to whether to use a narrative or key messages within a communication plan. The two are both about the words that sum up the situation and the response but are used in different ways. A narrative is a short passage of about three paragraphs that explains the position and provides a short story about what has happened and is going to happen. It is a brief overview that emphasizes the points that matter to the business. A set of key messages, however, is a series of bullet points that sum up what the business wants to say about the situation. There are strengths and weaknesses to each approach and the communicator may decide to use one or the other or in certain circumstances both. They are both used to underpin the activity that is going to be taken in response to the issue that has emerged.

Avoid the clichés

Key messages can become a series of overused statements and phrases that risk being ignored or seen as a 'cut and paste' statement failing to take account of the detailed circumstances. They do support consistency of messaging, however, as they provide clarity about what is being said. In contrast, a narrative can be open to interpretation, which some brands or businesses may find challenging. But the paragraphs provide a foundation that allows those responding to put the message into their own words. For example, those replying to stakeholders will use different words than someone putting together a social media response. The two need to come from the same narrative but can, and should, use words, phrases and sentences that are meaningful to the intended audience.

Deciding on whether to use a narrative or key messages in the development of a communication plan for the issue will depend on a number of things. Firstly, it will be linked to the extent, severity and seriousness of the issue or incident. If it is going to impact on a number of people, organizations, individuals, stakeholders and others then it may be that both are required. Secondly, if the situation could develop and run for a significant period of time then a narrative may be more beneficial to keep the focus on the fundamental points of the situation rather than to continually update a list of key messages. Thirdly, the people involved in the response may be unfamiliar with how to make effective use of a narrative and may be more comfortable adapting a list of key messages. It is important to consider how and who will be using the key messages or narrative. And finally, what level of action is going to be taken? Is the intervention going to be significant as it may require more detailed messaging to support the work?

Remember that while words and the messaging do matter, they are nothing without a strong organizational response to the issue or incident. A lack of action, or a failure to take a complaint or issue seriously, will be quickly identified despite any messaging that may present a contrary picture. Ensuring that the communication is an accurate reflection of the organization's position is critical to effective management of issues. This is why organizations require an issues management structure and approach to be in place throughout the business. Communication is a central player within this and will be among the first departments within an organization that will be involved with detailing the response. In many cases it will be the communication team that alert the business to an emerging issue and therefore trigger the activation of the issues management procedure.

The principles of intervention

It is important to be clear about the approach that is going to be taken to respond to the problem that has emerged. This will require answering some practical questions but also should take account of the Five Principles of Intervention. These principles underpin all the work that is undertaken to manage the issue and develop communication. From the moment that an issue is identified, the actions, activity and decisions should ensure that the principles are adhered to:

1 Visibility

2 Accountability

3 Proactivity

4 Responsiveness

5 Resolution

Visibility

It is important to demonstrate action to consider or rectify the situation. This may not always be in public as some issues will be highlighted to the business but will not feature in the media or on social media. They should not be treated any differently in terms of responding. But those involved or concerned about the issue should be able to see some form of response or activity related to the situation. For example, if there is a complaint about a product or service that is made through an email or letter it should receive the same consideration and care that would be taken with a response to a similar complaint made through social media.

Accountability

The business needs to take responsibility for the situation. If they are at the centre of an issue or incident that has developed, then they should be at the centre of the intervention or response. A business that waits for someone or another organization to step in and formulate the response will always be at a disadvantage when trying to manage a situation. They will struggle to manage what is happening and will be reacting to events after they have happened rather than taking the initiative and acting. For example, a data breach that the organization is alerted to should lead to the instigation of the issues management procedure to ensure the business is responding. Even if the breach is investigated by a third party, action can and should still be taken by the organization. However, it may need to be authorized by the third party.

Proactivity

Organizations should take action that will either bring the issue or incident to a swift conclusion or prevent the situation developing and causing increased damage. Managing the situation in a positive way can limit the damage to the business on many levels including reputationally and financially. It means early intervention is a priority, as is seeking to bring the issue to a swift conclusion, preventing further damage. For example, a complaint made on social media could be managed by a proactive response that shows action being taken both to review the situation and then consider next steps.

Responsiveness

Being responsive means taking account of all the information that exists and turning it quickly into an intervention. The details of what interventions can be made will be looked at later in this chapter. Organizations that are slow to react and act can be seen negatively by those involved in the issue or incident. At worst they can appear disinterested and dismissive of the problem and at best they appear incompetent. For example, a complaint may be easily rectified by providing a replacement product or a voucher. But if this takes weeks to agree and then offer it will allow the issue to grow and expand with frustration from those involved because of a lack of action.

Resolution

The aim of issue or incident management should not be just to protect the reputation of the business involved. It should be about finding a resolution to the issue or incident that has developed and bringing it to a satisfactory conclusion. If possible, this will be done so that not only does it meet the expectations of those involved but it exceeds them. The reputation of a brand or business can be improved by the way it goes beyond what is expected or required in dealing with an issue or incident. It can even mean a negative is turned into a positive by the response and the associated communication. For example, the customer complaint that is listened to, acted upon, replied about and resolved satisfactorily within a short space of time can create a positive impression of the organization.

Understanding the situation

In the initial stages of an issue emerging, it is important to continue to gather the details of what has happened, what impact it has had, and how it is developing. As discussed in Chapter 2, it is essential to have the data and insight about the issue and to track it as the situation develops and more information becomes available. Understanding what is currently happening and being able to predict or assess what could follow will support the intervention that is taken. It will also assist in supporting a change in the direction of the intervention if necessary. Having the best picture of the situation will support effective decision making on the next steps to take. Consider what you know is fact about the situation and make a clear differentiation between facts and speculation. It is important to see both so that you can plan for what may happen given the current circumstances. But be clear that this is based on supposition so is a case of it may happen rather than it definitely will. Actions need to be taken based on facts but with a consideration of potential future developments and scenarios.

In considering the situation, look at what you can learn from past experiences that may be relevant to the issue and particularly to future scenarios. If you have had similar issues affect the organization in the past, then ensure you have gathered the learning of what worked and what did not so that you can avoid repeating past mistakes. It is why debriefs and capturing learning about all issues and problems is so important. This is not just something to help the team today and in the next few weeks, but it should also be useful for new recruits and future employees. The approach that is taken needs to take account of the past, the present and the potential future for the issue and the organization.

Planning for what may happen

Scenario planning is one of the most important aspects of issues management. It is a chance to take a moment, take a deep breath and to then consider all your options in a calm and rational way. Getting a moment to step away from the emerging problem can feel challenging but brings huge benefits to the overall response. This does not have to be a long, drawn-out discussion, a day-long meeting or a drain on limited resources. Instead, it should be a focused look at the facts you have about the situation, the history of the business and any previous similar situations, a consideration of the external or internal discussion about the issue, and any data and insight that exists. Reviewing all this information in a calm atmosphere will give you the clarity to plan the way forward. The planning should consider what might happen next, where may this go, how may it develop, who else may become involved, and what additional risks have been identified.

It is also a moment where you can seek an impartial viewpoint on the situation that has developed or the issue that has emerged. Many organizations will have non-executive directors, customer panels and similar groups that they can consult with about the organization's development. Such groups can also be useful when looking at issue and incident management within the business. They should be involved in the review of what took place and what lessons can be learned at the resolution of the situation. They can also be asked to review plans and communication approaches that are being considered. Getting different perspectives on the situation and the planned response will strengthen the approach that is being taken and can identify gaps or aspects of concern. If such panels do not exist, then consider stakeholder groups or others outside the business that you could consult. The final resort would be to utilize social media data and information, although this will only give a view from those involved in digital commentary.

> TOP TIP
>
> Give yourself a moment away from the office, the ringing phones, the growing list of emails, and the pressure, and step out of the situation. It may help to block some time where you and colleagues, if possible, will be able to review the information and start to consider the way forward.

There are a number of questions to consider when reviewing the situation. These will help to ensure the details of the issue or problem are gathered before moving to decide how to respond. It is important to answer them with as much detail as possible and to recognize where gaps may exist. It ensures decision making is based on reliable information, which means a response is more likely to be effective:

1 **What is the current situation regarding the issue?**

    It is critical, as mentioned earlier, to have the latest information about the problem and what has happened. This can be assisted by putting an impact assessment in place. The impact analysis will consider the severity of the situation and how widespread it is for both operational and communication teams. An impact assessment will draw together all the data and information and requires this to be analysed for how seriously it affects the business, customers and others.

2 **At what speed is the situation growing?**

    It is vital to consider the speed at which things are developing as this may require a short route to planning a course of action. In situations where the problem is growing quickly, the need to act must be at the forefront of the communication planning. It will also require fast understanding of what is occurring and what it may become.

3 **Are people becoming aware of the problem and are they being critical of the business?**

    The more discussion is taking place about the problem then the more serious the situation may potentially become. When this discussion is becoming, or is currently, negative about the business it will require a swift but carefully managed response.

4 What impact has the situation had to date?

If the situation has already had a widespread impact on certain groups, then it may require action to be taken urgently. If people are broadly unaware of the issue, then the communicator has more time to analyse the situation and develop plans accordingly. This together, with question 3, which considers who is aware of, or impacted by, the situation, are critical questions to answer.

5 Are there any associated problems that could become linked to the issue?

The broader background and environmental scanning are important to consider in relation to the issue. If there are other issues or problems that the organization is managing, then these need to be understood and considered in relation to the emerging problem. The response made to one problem could negatively impact on another issue, on people, or on the wider business. But also, is there something happening in the world that may be linked to your developing situation?

6 Does the situation involve someone or something that is high profile?

The notoriety of the business, the issue, or someone linked to the problem could all lead to it attracting more attention, either from the media or people on social media. Such elements will require careful handling to minimize inflaming the situation.

7 Can you respond outside public awareness?

This is a critical question to consider. Are you able to deal directly with the complainant or whoever has raised concerns about the issue? If there is a possibility of dealing directly with them rather than operating through media or social media this is preferable, as it can bring earlier resolution. If there is media or social media interest that happens later this will be reflecting on a concluded and rectified situation, which will be more positive for the business's reputation.

8 **Does the issue link to any event, incident or situation in the past?**
If the latest problem is linked to previous issues, situations or problems then it adds a new dimension to the discussion. Instead of this being a one-off problem to consider it becomes an organizational or institutional failure. There will be additional questions about why this was not dealt with so that the problem could not re-emerge, and accusations levelled at those in charge.

Being able to accurately answer these questions should support the development of a detailed understanding of the situation. From that point the creation of a narrative and the move to consider the relevant intervention will be easier to determine. Interventions will change depending on the circumstances and as the situation develops the action that is taken should be refined and developed in response. Use the questions at any point in managing the issue to consider what may have changed or evolved with the problem, issue or incident. Remember that the situation will not remain static and unchanged. There may be external influences, environmental factors or public commentary that emerge and require a review of the action that is being taken. Internal influencers can also be in place and action from senior leaders or commentary from frontline staff may require a change in direction for the communication activity.

Ten interventions to respond to an issue

There are broadly 10 ways that an organization could respond to an issue once an initial assessment has been made. As mentioned, it is vital to keep the situation under review to decide whether any change in approach may be required. One or more of the interventions can be used at the same time.

1. Ignore the situation

In some cases, it may be valuable to watch what happens and decide the moment at which to take action, undertake further action or take a different approach. Action may not be required or may not need to be undertaken in a public format. It is a risky approach to take as the organization may get caught out and end up in a defensive position, being forced to react to what has happened. They can appear uncaring and disinterested in the issue that has occurred. Waiting to decide when to act is different to staying silent and hoping that the issue will go away or that the incident will resolve on its own.

2. Direct private response

It may be appropriate to respond to the issue that has been raised by making a direct approach to the individual or individuals that highlighted or raised it. This needs to be done in a spirit of openness and with a desire to listen and understand the concerns and the detail of the problem. This will allow action to be taken directly with the complainant or to gain a clearer understanding if other action is required. For example, a complaint about poor service would see the person contacted directly to find out what has happened, rectify any issues raised, and also consider if there is wider action that needs to be taken to avoid further complaints.

3. Internal organizational action

Once details of the issue are known and understood it may highlight that there is some form of organizational action or change required. A problem with a product may show that there is an issue in a manufacturing process. Listening to the concern can alert to the need to act. If there are concerns about the way employees are operating, then it may demonstrate that additional training is required. Undertaking internal action will usually be accompanied by another intervention, either direct or indirect, with those who have raised the issue.

4. Direct public response

When the issue emerges in a very public arena either through the news media or on social media, then the response requires some form of publicly shared intervention. If a conversation develops without intervention it can impact on the reputation of the organization as the business appears disinterested. Even if there is the opportunity to take conversations offline it is still important to ensure there is a public comment that demonstrates action is being taken behind the scenes.

5. Indirect public response

In some cases, the issue does not have an individual that can be easily identified to develop a direct line of communication. It may be that the situation emerges, and this requires some form of public statement to be made in an open forum. The purpose will be to ensure that all those affected by the issue know where to go, what to do and how to rectify the situation. For example, if there is a product failure that means many people may be affected or have issues, then a public response using a range of communication channels will provide those involved with details of how to rectify the situation.

6. Apology, either public or private

When there is an obvious failure that the company or organization has a significant responsibility for then an early apology can make a huge different to the outcome of the situation. If there is a public discussion about the situation, then finding a way to make a public response and apology can limit further criticism. In situations where problems emerge, and a direct approach is taken, then a private apology and offer to rectify the situation when undertaken in an authentic way can lead to a resolution. Making an apology before you are forced to is a technique known as 'stealing thunder': '*Stealing thunder* is a proactive crisis communication strategy by which an organization releases crisis information before media gets a hold of the crisis.'[1]

7. Managed escalation

In this approach there is a carefully managed plan where each development is reviewed and considered and, where appropriate, further action taken. The actions are introduced as required in a reactive strategy. This intervention is like playing a game of chess. With each move or situation that takes place there is a review of the escalation plan and a consideration of what further action may be necessary. There is little room to be proactive in this approach but it does ensure that there is no overreaction to the situation.

8. Divert attention

If the issue has attracted limited attention, then an organization can attempt to diminish the impact further by encouraging the focus to be placed on other areas. It may be an unconnected development or announcement, or something that minimizes the significance of the situation. Employing this intervention needs to be carefully handled as it can be heavily criticized as an attempt to evade dealing with the situation.

9. Third-party response and endorsement

Where an organization or body other than the one under pressure because of an emerging problem can make a response, it can be viewed as having more integrity and authenticity. There is often criticism that organizations are attempting to protect themselves through careful management of media and communication rather than dealing with the issue raised. In some cases, an intervention to address the problem, talk about action, or demonstrate a response can be made by bodies such as a board or non-executive directors, or an external organization. For example, a complaint about a failure by an organization may be proactively addressed by a board member who would be viewed as having independence in their response.

10. Move to crisis response

Where the situation continues to develop, intensifies or there are additional concerns and problems raised, it may become necessary to move to a crisis communication response. If early interventions have not made an impact, then more significant action may be needed. When the issue is spreading and impacting across the business or even further then the systems, processes and approaches of a crisis communication plan are required.

In deciding on the intervention that is required, whether to act or not, and what escalation plan to put in place it is vital to have situational awareness and perspective that can inform the decisions that are taken. In the initial stages of a problem emerging, look at the implications and the options for communication activity to step in and assist in achieving a resolution. One way to do this is to try to think forward and look at what may happen. Imagine that the problem has grown and pressure on the business has increased. What does this now sound like? What does it look like? Who is talking about the situation? What is it that they are talking about? Where is the media interest and what does that look like? Is there interest on social media and what is that like? Has there been third-party commentary? If this is an internal issue, has it reached outside the organization? If it is an external issue, has it had an impact on the employees?

The key in reviewing these and other questions is to consider the span of impact that the problem may have if it is able to grow and develop. Consider where this reaches into, whether that is across the business, with customers, with stakeholders or into other businesses. Assess where the biggest impact may be and who is likely to be the most affected if this situation develops. This will assist in then identifying the initial intervention that may be required and follow-up activity to implement should the situation develop.

TOP TIP

Words matter and it is helpful to build a document that focuses on words and phrases that should be used as well as those to avoid when managing problem situations. For example, avoid phrases such as 'learning the lessons' which mean nothing, and focus on words that are positive, compassionate and show action being taken.

Inclusivity within intervention

In considering how to address a problem it is important to ensure that your thinking is as broad as possible. The views and perspectives of those linked to the issue need to be understood and that is helped by creating an inclusive response. The challenge of inclusivity and understanding diversity is usually the preserve of the day-to-day communication to promote businesses and organizations. When dealing with problems, or even responding to an incident, the priority often becomes to act rather than to prepare and develop the response as outlined in the 10 interventions.

Start by asking if you really know who is involved and affected by the issue that has emerged. People can be restricted in their thinking by their own background and experience, which can limit their understanding of anything outside it. It is important not to assume anything and to challenge your understanding and thinking. For example, during the early days of the Covid-19 pandemic the UK Government used messages and channels that were later found to be failing to resonate with Black and Asian communities.[2] They were developing approaches from a white UK perspective, which had a focus on mainstream media and social media. However, they were not sources of information for those from other communities. The aim was to communicate the Covid-19 health advice to everyone, but this could not be achieved by relying on a specific set of channels.

Recognizing the challenge of developing inclusive communication is just the first step to effectively addressing the situation. What matters is taking action to review the approach to communication, particularly the messaging and channels that are used, and then to act to address any gaps within the response and the interventions being considered. There are a range of approaches that can be taken and should be considered to benefit all forms of communication activity.

Firstly, a third-party review may assess whether there is any problem with the proposed response. Identifying the most appropriate individual or group will be the challenge to undertaking this, as they may advise on how to respond to just some of the gaps that exist. However, a panel of experts drawn from across communities can improve this approach and be used to review communication strategies and plans. Having such a panel in place can inform communication approaches and increase understanding of communities and individuals, which can then be reflected in interventions and activity. In the event of a quick response being required, individuals or the whole panel can be asked for their views with a quick call or email.

Building your own understanding and knowledge about diversity and inclusive communication is essential. It means considering others' views and perspectives on situations and learning about what matters to those outside your experience and understanding. This assists in avoiding misunderstandings and miscommunication about the issue or incident. Reading on the subject is important but there are also experts in the communication field who provide valuable advice and information in this area. Webinars and training are also ways to develop but so is listening to others and what they are really saying. Understanding cultural differences is a huge subject area and there is a growing body of work looking at how to consider what it means for communication. Developing the response and approach to issues and incidents must be done with this in mind if it is to lead to an effective intervention.

When involving others in reviewing and developing the response, step outside the organization's and your own bubble to find the right people. Decision making is enhanced when you look more broadly at the issue or subject. As mentioned earlier, having a detailed understanding of the situation is essential when considering the interventions that may be required. When involving others in the work to broaden your understanding, consider five key questions:

1 Who do you need to, or want to, involve? Consider the knowledge and experience that you would benefit from and how it can support your communication activity.

2 Why do you want to involve them? This has to be about more than a 'PR exercise' that is being seen as doing the right thing. The advice must be considered and responded to.

3 How will you develop the communication activity? Consider the ways that the advice and guidance can be incorporated into the response. It is important to review the governance that exists around communication. Ensure external voices can be heard.

4 When will they be involved? Review at what point in the emergence of a problem or issue you will seek guidance from the group or individuals. Systems may need to be put in place to ensure a swift engagement or it may be required as the situation escalates.

5 What remit will they have? Ensure the role of the group or individuals is clear and that they know what they are being asked to do.

Engaging advice in practice

There are a number of practical considerations to engaging specialist advice and support to ensure you develop inclusive communication. First, there may be security implications for the business when sharing sensitive information with people outside the organization. This should not prevent the introduction of external perspectives, but it requires systems to be put in place that allow special advisers to have the necessary access. Depending on the level of access people will have they may need to undergo vetting or some form of security check or they may need to sign a confidentiality agreement. Ensure that these measures are appropriate to the level of access and are not overbearing, which may become a block to people wanting to get involved.

The recruitment of individuals for an advisory role should be undertaken objectively so that there is no bias built into the process. Build a network that can provide this support to the organization as required. A citizen panel, or communication advisory group, whatever you decide to call it is not important – what matters is that they can bring a different perspective to the situation, the response and the communication.

Ensure that advisers are independent and feel supported to freely speak their minds and comment honestly on the communication and approach being considered. They should not be an established part of the organization as this will limit their effectiveness. If payment is given it should be appropriate to the activity but clearly not as a paid employee. The ability to remain impartial after working with, or advising, an organization over a number of years is challenging. People can build relationships, make connections and foster loyalties that previously did not exist. This can consciously or subconsciously affect their commentary and capacity to remain impartial. One option is to recruit people for a fixed term so that they can be involved for a limited five or ten years. However, if you involve them infrequently then it may not be required as they will not build the connection to the organization.

Using imagery and supporting material

This chapter has focused on the importance of words and messaging to the intervention and response, but imagery is also a key element. Whether it is photography, illustration or video, they all enhance and support the communication response to an issue, incident or emerging problem. Organizations that understand and can utilize the visual in their proactive communication can bring it into a response to challenging situations. Imagery can be used to highlight a particular position, to demonstrate the work that the organization is doing to deal with the issue, or to provide a little humour to the situation. It is important to carefully consider the use of humour before involving it in your response. There are occasions when it can defuse a tense situation or show the personality of the brand or business. For example, consider the response from Kentucky Fried Chicken when they had to close stores because they ran out of chicken. The problem in 2018 led to them putting adverts into newspapers to apologize, featuring an image of an empty KFC bucket with the letters re-arranged to say FCK. This was a risky response but was in line with the brand image of the business.[3]

The importance of social media in modern communication has necessitated the ability to produce impactful and engaging content. When dealing with everyday problems communicators have to use more than just words. The use of images can draw attention to the organization's position and increase the reach of the messaging. Video of someone in the organization giving a verbal statement, images of the organization directly dealing with the problem, and even stock photography can all be used to enhance the response. Social media and digital developments have increased the need for more than just words to build an effective response. Video, audio, podcasts and more have all expanded the options available. It is not a requirement to use them in every situation, but they should be considered as ways of enhancing the communication interventions.

But as with the messages that are developed, it is important to ensure that they are likely to be effective and that they will not create a further problem. Consider whether the supporting material you are going to use could be insensitive, upsetting, or inappropriate. From the perspective of the communication team, it may be impactful and engaging but those affected by the problem may take a different view. As with the wording, an external adviser or panel can be used to consider the implications of the approach being taken and ensure it is inclusive.

Assessing the intervention

Before implementing a course of action, the approach should be considered from a number of perspectives. This will help to assure the quality of the plan and the communication that has been outlined.

In order to do this effectively the communicator should have a good understanding of the organization, the market in which it operates, and the risks that it faces. This will ensure a good knowledge of the wording and imagery that may be acceptable to use and that support the brand identity. They must also keep up to date with developments within the business or the industry in which it operates to ensure that the interventions are still appropriate. Beyond all the specific knowledge of the business, communicators must also be aware of societal changes and developments that may impact on any aspect of their work. For example, criticism about an organization's environmental credentials may have been seen as not a priority in the 1980s but more recently it has become a critical issue for businesses. The response to criticism now would be quite different to 40 years ago.

The following checklist can be used to help review the approach and show if there are any gaps in what is being proposed. If gaps in knowledge and understanding are identified the plan for intervention can be reviewed, refined and developed to address the omission.

CHECKLIST

1 Have a plan. If there is already one, then review what it says about the action to take.

2 Develop a clear narrative and messages to explain the situation with clarity.

3 Focus the approach on an active response and what is being done about the situation.

4 Review earlier incidents. Look for documents or feedback about what did and did not work.

5 Get a third-party review of the approach being developed. Use a customer panel or independent adviser to consider all perspectives.

6 Discuss the approach with employees. Use either an internal panel or key, informed contacts within the business to gauge their views.

7 Assess feedback, particularly online messages, for similar responses. Gather information from surveys and activity.

8 Use images and supporting material. Enhance the communication message with additional elements.

9 Identify the potential ways the issue could develop and consider the escalation of communication activity in response.

10 Consider what is happening in the business that may affect the response.

11 Review the external factors that may impact on the effectiveness of the actions to manage the issue.

12 Ensure close monitoring of the impact that both the issue and the communication response are having.

CASE STUDY

What happened?

In February 2021 there were two situations that emerged which demonstrated the importance of choosing the right words in the right place at the right time. They both had a significant impact and created issues that needed careful management. In the first case the UK chair of accountancy firm KPMG told staff to 'stop moaning'[4] about the Covid-19 pandemic and also to stop 'playing the victim card'.[5] The message by Bill Michael was given while talking on a virtual meeting with 1,500 staff. Despite an apology to staff an independent investigation into the comments was launched and just days later he quit his role, saying the position had become 'untenable'.[6] In the same week that this happened to Mr Michael, the president of the Tokyo 2020 Olympic Games resigned following sexist remarks he had made.[7] He was quoted as saying that women talk too much 'which is annoying'.[8] Yoshiro Mori later retracted his comments, adding 'I don't listen to women that much lately, so I don't know'.[9] He resigned a few days later after an emergency meeting of the committee to consider what had happened.

In both cases the choice of words led to an issue being created. In the case of Yoshiro Mori, the reported comments that he made in an attempt to respond to the situation made the position worse. They show why it is critical to consider the intervention, words, imagery and elements from a range of perspectives. Both these situations show the importance of training senior managers and leaders in communication and not just in dealing with the media. The people at the top of organizations face significant pressure to ensure they use the right words and images at the right time. Communicators can assist in ensuring this happens through training, keeping senior people in touch with the ground floor business, and bringing views and perspectives from others into the boardroom.

There are many interviews, comments, meetings and emails that are sent across businesses every day. The probability that a business will face a similar situation at some point, where the wrong phrase, words or sentiments are made by those in a senior position, is extremely high. There is an opportunity to consider the approaches that will be taken and responses that may be given before any such problem emerges.

KEY LEARNING POINTS

- Train those at the top of the business in all forms of communication from addressing stakeholders through to speaking to staff and customers. Media training is not enough as it is only part of the work leaders do in communicating.

- Keep senior leaders in touch with what is happening within the business. Encourage them to spend time on the frontline of the organization with what are often called 'back to the floor' days.

- Develop opportunities where customers/service users and staff can meet the decision makers within the business to share their views.

- Encourage the independent panel that supports the development of inclusive communication to talk with those at the top of the business to share their perspectives.

- Be aware of the potential responses, media and social media angles to every speech, commentary and interview that is given. This will prevent errors in judgement and stop such problems before they happen.

- Plan for a reputational problem to emerge. The issues and incidents that face communicators every day are often rooted in words, views and commentary about a product or business. Think through the interventions that may be deployed to address such situations.

Conclusion

The words that are used to respond to a situation are critical and can mean the difference between containing the issue early and seeing it develop into a crisis. It is essential that the communicator begins with a clear and detailed understanding of the problem, what it means, why it has happened and who is involved. This information will allow an intervention plan to be created that identifies what options can be taken and at what point they may be used. Developing this further into an escalation plan will provide a readiness to be able to respond quickly to changing events.

Creating a narrative and key messages underpins all communication activity. Take care to work this out and choose the words with care, paying attention to how they may be viewed from outside the organizational bubble. This can be supported with imagery and additional material to enhance the response and increase the impact that it can have. Words and supporting materials matter and ensuring the approach is inclusive and recognizes differences in culture is essential. Failing to take care and or to have the communication response reviewed by experts and independent advisers may create a further problem for the business. An organization could quickly find they have two problems to manage: the initial situation and the one created by inappropriate language or messaging.

Making the right intervention requires the communicator to have a good understanding of the way media and social media operate. The activity may need to be developed and adapted to make the most of the opportunities from social media or to be able to effectively deal with the potential media angles. The details of how to do this will be covered in the next two chapters.

Notes

1   Yeal Lee, S (2016) Weathering the crisis: Effects of stealing thunder in crisis communication, *Public Relations Review*, www.sciencedirect.com/science/article/abs/pii/S0363811115301661#:~:text=Stealing%20thunder%20as%20a%20crisis%20communication%20strategy%20involves%20revealing%20negative,et%20al.%2C%201993) (archived at https://perma.cc/H65M-CZML)

2   Lawrence, D (2020) An Avoidable Crisis: The disproportionate impact of Covid-19 on Black, Asian and minority ethnic communities, www.lawrencereview.co.uk (archived at https://perma.cc/JT9E-LJFM)

3   Oster, E (2018) KFC responds to UK chicken shortage scandal with a timely 'FCK, We're sorry', *Adweek*, 23 February, www.adweek.com/creativity/kfc-responds-to-u-k-chicken-shortage-scandal-with-a-timely-fck-were-sorry/ (archived at https://perma.cc/479T-ZXWH)

4   Sweney, M and Partridge, J (2021) KPMG's Bill Michael resigns after telling staff to 'stop moaning', *Guardian*, 12 February, www.theguardian.com/business/2021/feb/12/kpmg-bill-michael-resigns-after-telling-staff-to-stop-moaning (archived at https://perma.cc/MVL2-RDVA)

5   Kapoor, M (2021) KPMG UK boss exits after slamming 'victim card' staff (1), *Bloomberg*, 12 February www.bloomberg.com/news/articles/2021-02-12/kpmg-chair-resigns-days-after-slamming-victim-card-staff#xj4y7vzkg (archived at https://perma.cc/3BTJ-PPZQ)

6   BBC News online (2021) KPMG boss Bill Michael quits after 'stop moaning' row, 12 February, www.bbc.co.uk/news/business-56038215 (archived at https://perma.cc/QGP9-HPMJ)

7   BBC News online (2021) Yoshiro Mori: Tokyo Olympics chief steps down over sexism row, 12 February, www.bbc.co.uk/news/world-asia-56020674 (archived at https://perma.cc/VD2B-QMR6)

8   BBC News online (2021) Yoshiro Mori: Tokyo Olympics chief steps down over sexism row, 12 February, www.bbc.co.uk/news/world-asia-56020674 (archived at https://perma.cc/VD2B-QMR6)

9   Sky News Online (2021) Tokyo Olympics chief Yoshiro Mori 'to step down' after saying women talk too much in meetings, 11 February, https://news.sky.com/story/tokyo-olympics-chief-yoshiro-mori-to-step-down-after-saying-women-talk-too-much-in-meetings-12214789 (archived at https://perma.cc/TT6K-T7ZN)

5

Working with the media

Introduction

Who are the news media?

The media have had a central position in managing the response to problems for many years. Back in the 16th century the first newspapers were being produced[1] and this continued for many centuries before they were joined by radio and then television broadcasts. From the 1980s the communication world expanded to include digital media with the development of online channels, social media, bloggers and virtual communication trends.[2] Throughout this time there has been fluctuating decline and growth in aspects of what we call the news media. The biggest change is the loss of traditional printed newspapers, which have been replaced by online channels, networks on Facebook, Twitter and TikTok, and hyperlocal news outlets. Mainstream media have been using social networks as a way to reach people. For example, the *Washington Post* is reaching out to new readers using the social media app TikTok.[3] In the UK it is estimated more than 260 local newspapers have disappeared since 2005,[4] while in the United States research in early 2022 found that the largest newspapers had lost 30 per cent of their print circulation in the previous two years.[5]

Modern technology allows anyone to take on the role of journalist, able to make comment on an issue and share photographs and videos. Live streaming is available to everyone using social media and these developments have changed the nature of relationships with the media. This includes a question about who the news media are and who communicators should prioritize working with. For brands and businesses, the impact of these hyperlocal sites, Facebook group pages, and citizen journalists may be more detrimental and potentially challenging to respond to than traditional news media reporting on an issue. This is because they are bound by no journalistic conventions and may even operate anonymously making it difficult for communicators to contact them and build relationships. This chapter will focus on the mainstream or traditional news media including how it operates in the digital space. The vital role of social media will be covered in Chapter 6.

The way people consume news has changed in line with the development of digital media. This has been a challenge for the relationships many organizations have with the news media; there is confusion about who are trained and reputable journalists and publications. Locally focused bloggers and citizen journalists can be overlooked by organizations when they should be part of the consideration in media handling. In many cases this may be because of a lack of understanding about the role that they play in the local community, or due to a concern about the limited resources that are available to focus on media engagement work.

The key place of news media in managing issues, incidents and emerging problems remains unchanged. They continue to have a sphere of influence and a place in modern life, including within the digital space. Understanding the news media is essential to managing emerging problems. Each news outlet will have different approaches and priorities, which may impact on the action that is taken, what is said, and how the communication is managed.

The news media work on three levels: local, national and international. In the world of social media where people are more connected than ever before, the ability for a story to spread around the world within a short space of time is evident. Most communicators usually deal with local news reporters and occasionally may be contacted by the national media. However, it is important to always recognize that the international media may become involved in reporting a story. The conventions of media operations differ from country to country. There will be written and unwritten rules about the way they work so it is important to understand what these are, particularly if you regularly work internationally. All communicators need to be ready to work with, and engage with, media from around the world if they become interested in an issue or incident you are managing.

Media interest

Understanding what is of interest to the news media is important and the communicator will benefit from some time working in a newsroom. This helps to understand how the news media operate, how they find and then select stories to cover, and the deadlines they work to. Spending some time looking at this supports the communicator in getting into the mind of the journalist. It will show what elements of a story are likely to bring news media attention and how a minor problem can become a major issue when it reaches a journalist's radar. News reporters are interested in the unusual, the new, and something that has made an impact on a local community or individual. The bigger the impact the more likely it is that the media will be interested and will start to ask questions. There are six elements that indicate the issue or incident that is being managed is likely to attract media interest.

1. Relevance

The news reporter will be interested in things that have a relevance either due to the geographic location of the issue, or because it is a critical subject that matters to readers, viewers or listeners. This is why the local newspaper is interested in events and news from local institutions such as schools and factories.

2. Unusual or unexpected

Events that are out of the ordinary or appear without any warning can draw interest from news reporters. The problem will stand out if it has not been seen or experienced before. A problem that has unique elements will be of note to the media. Organizations and businesses that suddenly behave in a way that is out of step with their usual brand values are of interest to journalists. For example, a business that is environmentally friendly will become newsworthy when they are found to be investing in ecologically damaging businesses.

3. Conflict and disagreement

The media regularly follow stories that are about a disagreement between two or more parties. Conflict is always of note and if this involves a David and Goliath scenario then the interest will be heightened. For example, a complaint about a product from a customer that is dismissed by the business may be taken to the media, who can visualize it as an opportunity for them to support the underdog against big business. This is why interventions at an early stage, as outlined in Chapter 4, can be so critical to managing an issue.

4. Celebrity or human interest

Any situation that involves famous or well-known people can attract media interest. Such people have a readily available platform to air their views either through the media – local, national or international – or by using their own accounts on social channels. They can be influencers on the situation. But even if the issue does not involve famous people, it can still make a news story if there is a strong and accessible human interest angle. Personal accounts of situations and issues have an authenticity and a connection to viewers and readers.

5. New

It may seem obvious to say that new things make the news but when events have not been seen before then they will be of interest to the media. When proactively promoting developments, this is beneficial. However, at moments when communicators are attempting to manage issues and incidents it can be unhelpful. For example, a new system being introduced or the launch of a new product is newsworthy.

6. Change

Developments and events that lead to a change within a business or organization will also be of interest to the media. Questions will be asked about why the change is required. Has there been a problem that has led to the decision? What was going wrong to require the business to change? While change can be implemented because of positive developments it is also seen as a recognition that something was not working well or as it should have been. This is why managing the communication of change is so critical to how it is viewed both inside and outside the business.

There may be other elements that attract media interest but these six, either individually or collectively, are signposts of potential challenges ahead. If an issue, development or problem is likely to touch these elements then ensure that a plan is developed so that the media and other interests can be proactively managed. Working effectively with the media is a key part of that, and many other communication plans.

Recognize the value of effective media relations. This relies on both an understanding of how the news media work and developing relationships with them. When a problem has emerged, businesses and brands often want to keep it out of the media and mistakenly think that failing to respond to them will achieve that. But if the issue is already being discussed by the media, on social media or in local communities, then working with the news media can bring significant benefits.

Building positive relationships

Working with the media can be seen as combative and part of a battle that has to be fought. When a business is facing a crisis and is under pressure this can emerge, but it is not a forgone conclusion. Managing problems and everyday issues can be a positive opportunity to work with local or selected news media. It is a chance to build relationships by being open and sharing details and updates. Consider what the organization wants to achieve in dealing with the issue. Remember the interventions outlined in Chapter 4 and review which may seem appropriate to the situation, then look at where discussion or contact with the relevant media who are interested in the situation can be beneficial to the aim and outcome.

In order that a business can move positively to manage a situation or problem it requires them to have existing relationships with the news media. These relationships cannot be created overnight and need to be part of daily activity within the communication team. When a situation emerges, there is little time and ability to develop trust between an organization and the media. Communicators can use social media, as has been said, but this cannot replace the news media and the role they have within society; it is significant and can create or expand a problem for an organization. There are four steps to building positive relationships with the news media.

Step 1: Understand your journalists

The starting point is to really understand the news media and journalists that are key to your business and the sector it operates within. Spend some time in identifying who they are and what aspects they are particularly interested in. These journalists may be in specialist media related to the industry or they may be linked to the geographic area. It may help to split them into primary and secondary media outlets. Primary are those that have weekly or monthly interest in the business, and secondary are those who have passing interest on a less frequent basis. Both are important and should be connected with, but more time and effort should be focused on those who are regularly contacting the business.

Step 2: Spend time with them

Once you have identified who the key journalists are, whether primary or secondary, it is important to learn about them and understand what they do. This involves spending some time with them if that is possible, in the newsroom or shadowing them at work. For communicators who are new to the industry and may not have journalism in their background this step is essential to expand their knowledge. Use this work to understand how the journalist and media outlet operate as well as what they do when they become aware of a potential story.

Step 3: Help them understand you

Once you have taken time to see how the journalist operates, this should be followed by making sure that they have a good basic knowledge of the business. When there is no problem or crisis looming, time can be spent opening up the business so that the media are educated about how it operates, the positive work that is underway, and key developments. This can be done through organizing a familiarization day where key people and areas of work are demonstrated to journalists. There should also be regular meetings with the CEO and top team to discuss developments and areas that can be proactively provided to the media. Meetings to showcase key areas of the business can assist in building knowledge of the business and relationships. It is important to remember that such events cannot be a one-off, as journalists will change, new publications may appear, and those at the top of the business may change. Keeping updated contacts lists and a focus on relationship building should happen every day.

Step 4: Keep in contact

Once Steps 1 to 3 have been carried out then the last step is to make regular connections with the key journalists. This does not always have to be linked to a story or development but should be to check what is of interest to them, what aspects may be coming into focus for the media outlet, or just to check in with them. It is through these connections that you can build trust and an understanding that can help at the time a problem emerges.

On some occasions a new journalist or new media outlet will come into contact with the business about a problem or issue and no prior work will have been done to build a relationship. In these situations, try to focus on having a positive discussion and approach to the line of questioning that is put forward. It may become an opportunity to make new connections. Whatever happens, resorting to a 'no comment' approach to the media is never beneficial. It makes the organization appear secretive and leads to mistrust with the media. There are other more effective approaches that can be taken which will be outlined later in this chapter when looking at responses that can be made to the news media.

The global media

Wherever you are in the world, working with media from overseas presents additional challenges for any organization or business. For the international business some of these issues can be managed through the relationships that are built day to day between communication teams or staff in different countries and their local media. But for many others there is a requirement to understand the ways in which the media work in different countries. This will include understanding the legislative framework that may affect how they operate, and any standards that are adhered to through local agreements. Both these elements can impact on the responses given and how relationships are built between businesses and the media.

Sensitivity to cultural differences is essential to building these relationships and to avoiding additional problems when responding to an emerging issue. Using the four-step approach should ensure that the details and way of operating in different countries and communities are identified and understood. At the heart of the work is the need to ensure that sharing information with the media is done in an inclusive way. Do not limit the work and the understanding to mainstream media. Understand the communities that you are connecting with and where they access news. It is those publications and broadcasts that should be contacted. As mentioned in the previous chapter it is easy to look from your own background or to focus on the mainstream, but this fails to develop an inclusive response. Be prepared for the possibility of overseas media interest and have a process in place to deal with it if it happens. Such international approaches are now more likely due to social media; small issues and problems can capture media interest and be covered globally in an instant.

TOP TIP

Investing in a media database can assist businesses by providing detailed information about news media at home and abroad. This information will help you to understand when you are contacted who the media outlet is, what areas they are interested in, the sphere of influence that they have, and other key data and information. Media databases also provide contact details that will allow you to be proactive in contacting the media.

Having information readily at hand is essential when improving the management of everyday issues and problems. If a situation escalates quickly the information needs to be instantly accessible and there may be little time, or spare resources, to allow detailed research on media outlets to be undertaken. To support the data gathering about international media, there are PR organizations that work internationally such as the International Public Relations Association[6] who can provide such information. Connecting with them may help to expand knowledge about media operations around the world or to connect with PR professionals in those countries who may be able to provide invaluable information.

Turning a negative into a positive

When managing an emerging problem, the aim is to approach it in a positive way and identify opportunities to reach a successful conclusion. But in some cases, the alert to a problem may initially come from the media who are asking questions about a change, complaint or other issue. At this point, the business can be put 'on the back foot', trying to quickly gather the information to be able to develop the required response. It may appear at this point that the media interest is highlighting a negative position in relation to the business. Work may be put in place to attempt to turn the negative situation into a more positive one for the organization. At the heart of any response is a need to be listening and, in this situation, listening to exactly what the media are saying or asking about. Avoid taking a defensive stance as this will appear to be an attempt to hide the reality of the situation or to protect the reputation of the organization at the expense of everything else. The media will attempt to break down such a position either by unearthing more information to confront the business with, by speaking to other people, or by revisiting the problem at a future date.

In an attempt to turn negative approaches into a positive response, be clear in recognizing what has happened. If the media are aware of something, attempting to deny there is any issue will at worst appear to be dishonest. Remember the information about interventions mentioned in Chapter 4 and see the situation from the position of those who have highlighted it. What does it look like to them? What does it mean to them and others? Understanding the reality for others will assist in clarifying the approach to take. Be open to what is being said by journalists, listen to it and understand it. The next step is to replay the position to others from the perspective of the business.

Explain the situation with an honest appraisal of what has happened and most importantly what is being done to address it. It is not a moment to be defensive, or to deny what is obviously happening. Speaking about the position the business has found itself in will help to provide some clarity on the story.

The media will try to undermine such a position by finding evidence to challenge the business with, by speaking to others to provide negative commentary, or by returning to the problem at a future date to assess the response. Whose voices will be the loudest? In the absence of information from the business, those watching, reading or listening to reports about the situation will make judgements based on partial information. Those judgements have the potential to impact on the reputation of the business and can lead to dwindling sales, lost confidence and a hit to the public standing of the organization. Take the opportunity to be clear about what the business understands about the situation and that it is being active to address the situation or the perceptions of it.

Keep the response human

The explanation needs to show that the business has been listening to the comments, complaints or issues that have been raised. As mentioned earlier, human interest stories are relished by the news media who will be looking at what individuals have to say about the situation. Make sure that your intervention and response does not neglect the human element. There will be many other competing demands on the communication response, whether it is sharing information with stakeholders or shareholders or managing the impact on sales, but in media and social media scrutiny the way people are dealt with will be paramount to perceptions of what has happened. Developing the response must ensure that the actions and communication are about people first and the brand and business's reputation second. This will be more effective in challenging negative commentary and news articles.

When faced with a negative news story avoid becoming angry about what is being said, even when it is potentially inaccurate or damaging to the business. A calm approach will always yield better results, and this will be discussed further in Chapter 7, which looks at effective decision making. For those leading companies it can feel like a personal attack when negative reporting is taking place, so it is a moment to step back, take a deep breath and look objectively at the situation. Only once this has been done should actions and plans be discussed and developed. It is also important to avoid being dismissive about the problem or issue that has been raised. For the business it may be a minor inconvenience or low-level problem, but for those affected by it the impact can be significant. Again, this is why viewing the situation from the perspective of those affected is important. Being dismissive can be potentially damaging to the reputation of the business. Some form of direct contact with those affected is always preferable as it demonstrates a willingness to listen and allows a discussion about the business's view of what has happened. This conversation may be about the business acknowledging that something has gone wrong and is being addressed, or an opportunity to clarify what the accurate position is and correct any misunderstanding. It is important to have carried out this direct connection so that it can be used to strengthen any media statement or response.

Turning things around takes time

When attempting to turn negative commentary into positive it is important to recognize that it cannot be done overnight and often will take some time before you get to the required position. The approach should start by considering the allegations or points that are being made about the situation and the business. Look at what the organization can say and do to present their position on the problem. This may require an initial intervention acknowledging that there will be a response provided in more detail at a future point, and also stating that the business is aware there is an issue ahead of creating a more detailed communication plan for the response. Rushing ahead may mean that incorrect comments are made, or that the business moves to rebut the position without a full understanding of what has happened or how it is developing. Take time to review the problem and consider the appropriate ways forward to engage with the media, to approach those affected by the situation, to be clear about what has happened, or not happened, and what the business is doing about it.

The approach may need to take small steps in the communication plan to effectively turn around a negative news media response. Deal with the perceptions people have of the business; just telling them they are wrong about the situation will not deal with their negative thoughts and views. The way forward will be to demonstrate what has happened, so they understand they have the wrong perception of the business. This explanation could be directly about the problem, or through using the proactive communication activity about broader subjects. Engaging with the media will be a part of this activity with other communication channels supporting the position as required to promote the positive position. The work that has been done building relationships with the media will be critical in moving from a negative to a positive position. Having developed links to key journalists this provides a direct line to be able to share the organization's position. This is not about pushing the media to report in a particular way or using pressure to prevent a story being run. Key media reporters should be contacted to explain the business's position and correct any inaccuracies about what is being said. Doing this is much easier when the communicator knows, or has already spoken to, the journalist.

Facing criticism

An example would be a group unhappy with the business for some reason who establish a Facebook page to criticize the brand on a regular basis. At first the media will not be aware of it, and as they do become aware it may lead them to ask questions. In the initial stages these may be passing questions about the business being aware of the page and trying to discover what they are doing about it. If the group grows and continues to share negative views of the business, then the media will report it and discuss with the organizers what they are doing and why. What could be done with this situation?

First, as soon as the organization becomes aware of the group being established it should prepare a media statement and answer any questions that may follow, either from reporters or through social media. At the same time, the communicator should understand what the problem is, who may be responsible, and what can and is being done about it. If possible, a direct approach to those behind the creation of the group would assist in understanding what the problem is, what additional issues may be raised, and what resolution they are hoping for. It also demonstrates an open and listening organization and could allow a swift intervention to limit the impact of the situation. If these discussions bring a resolution, it can avoid the involvement of the media, or if they are already aware it may reduce the impact of any articles. Speaking directly with those affected can avoid the media becoming involved in any delicate negotiations.

Finally, if the media are aware of the group, then explaining the situation from the business's perspective, detailing any actions now and for the future, and demonstrating a positive response, can support an effective response. Remember to use social media as part of the response as this is where the issue originated. The news media and social media now operate very closely together and are entwined within issues management. Engaging with the Facebook group and using social media to respond should be considered as part of the communication response. The role of social media will be discussed in more detail in Chapter 6.

Tactics when working with the media

There are three main approaches when considering how to work with the media in managing the response to an issue or problem: stay silent, say something, or go proactive. Deciding which approach to take will depend on the details of the issue being managed, what else may be happening, and how the situation is, or may be, developing. The interventions outlined in Chapter 4 can assist in considering what approach to take with the media at what stage of the issue being managed.

1. Staying silent

This could be saying 'no comment' when approached by the media about a problem that has emerged but there are other ways that a business can remain quiet while being positive. A lack of media engagement may allow direct contact to be made with those who are complaining or have been affected. This allows the first media interaction to be to state that the issue has been effectively resolved. However, saying nothing does not have to be a permanent state. It can be a position taken for a limited amount of time to allow for contact as mentioned above or to ensure the full information about the situation has been uncovered. Communicators must take care in taking the approach of remaining silent as it can be used against the business. It can allow inaccuracies to spread, commentary about the organization failing to take things seriously to circulate, or can be seen as arrogance. If staying silent is used with the media, ensure a quick intervention can be made if needed to prevent the story escalating unnecessarily.

2. Saying something

If approached by the media about an issue, then providing some information or a limited response may be the least risky way forward. It demonstrates that the organization is aware of the problem and can show that action of some form is being taken. Effectively it gives a position that can be built upon whether the issue develops or not. Providing a basic comment will allow the business some time to understand the detail of what has happened or what is being alleged. It is important to recognize that this time may be quite limited depending on what that situation is. Being able to move quickly to say more about what has happened and what is being done is crucial. The media always follow up stories and there will inevitably be further questions to answer about what has happened since the initial discussion or comment was made. Never assume that saying something to allow some time will mean the end of the media questioning in relation to the situation.

3. Going proactive

In some cases, the situation may be clear, and the organization may have detailed knowledge of what has happened. If something has gone wrong, they will know why and what is being put in place to deal with it. At this point it can be most effective to proactively approach the media to discuss the changes that are being made. The detail of the problem will be mentioned but the focus can be on what the organization has done or is doing to address things. This can take the sting out of some problems and situations. It does require an open, honest and accountable approach to communication. The business needs to be prepared to talk openly about what happened and to accept responsibility if there were things that should have been done differently. It also requires the business to have good relationships with the media so they can approach them directly to share the details of the situation and the action.

When to complain

Despite your best efforts to forge positive working relationships with journalists there will be moments when there is a significant disagreement, and you may feel compelled to complain. In most cases it is leaders within organizations that want to resort to complaint or formal redress when they feel the media have been 'unfair' to the business. Complaints should be a last resort after negotiations with journalists have failed, or when an article has been inaccurate or potentially damaging from a legal perspective by being either libellous or slanderous. The starting point should be understanding if there is a potential for serious inaccuracy to be contained within the media story. Communicators need to take all available steps to try to ensure that the inaccuracy is corrected, preferably ahead of publication or broadcast.

Speak to the journalist and provide information to clarify the position and point out the inaccuracies within the comments they have made or the article they are developing. Remember that this needs to be inaccurate commentary and not just something that the business doesn't like, or perceptions that they disagree with. In this latter situation, seek to provide an alternative viewpoint that helps to correct the perception through the statement and any interviews that are given. If there is a serious inaccuracy and the journalist is unwilling or uninterested in your attempt to clarify the position, then speak to the news editor or editor. Before taking this higher, be clear what is incorrect and what needs to be done to clarify the position. As they are not directly involved in the news gathering, they are often in a position to take a more reasonable position even if this still means the article will be published or broadcast.

Legal action or referring the situation to a regulatory body should be a last resort when all other methods of challenging the inaccuracy have failed. It can be costly and difficult to prevent an article being broadcast and usually the situation will leak out in some way unless there is a detailed injunction in place. However, the move can be taken with the support of legal representatives, while also recognizing the long-term damage this will do to relationships with the media organization. The following steps can help to rectify problems before they need to be made more formal:

1 Attempt to explain to the journalist ahead of publication or broadcast.

2 Speak to the news editor or editor about the problem ahead of publication or broadcast.

3 Ask for an apology and correction if the article is published or broadcast.

4 Refer the issue to the Independent Press Standards Organization (IPSO) or Ofcom in the UK, or the equivalent regulator in other countries.

5 Seek legal advice to either stop the article being published or to challenge once it has been published.

CASE STUDY

What happened?

In August 2021, the UK was experiencing a shortage of lorry drivers which was being created by a number of problems including the Covid-19 pandemic and people leaving their jobs. The impact of the problems in the supply chain was that some takeaways and restaurants had a shortage of available food to sell. Among those affected were some McDonald's fast food restaurants and Costa Coffee shops. The issue was highlighted to the media a week earlier when Nando's closed an estimated 50 restaurants because of food shortages.[7] This time lag allowed other food outlets to consider their position and determine if there were problems likely to occur. A fast food restaurant without food will always be a story of interest to the media. But the fact that the issue had already been highlighted gave others including McDonald's and Costa Coffee the ability to show they were not outliers but were in a similar position. This would prevent them being singled out for criticism because of the problem itself occurring.

McDonald's provided a statement to the media that sought to align them with other retailers, to try to show the issue had only limited impact, while also apologizing and showing action was being taken. Part of the statement said: 'Like most retailers, we are currently experiencing some supply chain issues, impacting the availability of a small number of products. Bottled drinks and milkshakes are temporarily unavailable in restaurants across England, Scotland and Wales. We apologize for any inconvenience and thank our customers for their continued patience.'[8] They were able to use the final line to speak directly to customers and show they understood the frustration that may be being felt.

At the same time, Costa Coffee was experiencing problems and the media were able to use a statement the company released on Twitter. The statement was a partial response that would allow the company to develop a more detailed response should it be required. Costa Coffee had a number of products that were unavailable because of the same distribution problems being felt by other retailers. The statement was brief but did show an awareness of the situation and a drive to resolve it swiftly. It said: 'We are facing some supply chain issues just now. We're working hard to resolve this ASAP.'[9] The media did pose further questions such as when the issues would be resolved but these were not directly aimed at the company in a negative way. With both organizations there was a decision that had to be made about whether or not to say something about the supply issues. Speaking about the problem may have placed the attention of a wider industry issue at their doorstep. But in both cases, it became an opportunity to show they were aware of the problem, were sorry about what had happened, and were actively addressing it. Ultimately, that prevented the situation developing into a crisis as it was confronted at an early stage in a proactive way.

KEY LEARNING POINTS

- Watch what is happening in the industry that the business operates within. This will ensure an awareness about a problem that may affect the business in the future.

- Get to know the news media that are important to your business. This will help in developing proactive plans to address an emerging issue. It can also support the building of relationships and networks to use in future situations.

- Understand the risks that the business may face and be prepared to act. Each business has a list of problems that could happen within its risk register. Being aware of these will improve the ability to spot situations before they develop. With McDonald's and Costa Coffee, preparing for a distribution problem would have allowed communication to be shared quickly before customers visited stores and found out for themselves.

- Detail your approach and the steps that will be taken both at the start of the problem and in the future. Costa Coffee should have been ready to say more about what had been done once the initial tweet had been sent out for the media to use.

- Ensure communicators have a good understanding of what makes news and how the media operate. This supports the preparation of effective communication plans using knowledge of the ways a story may be handled.

- Social media can support your news media activity as the two are interconnected. Costa Coffee demonstrated how Twitter was able to support their media management when the statement was picked up and used in articles.

Conclusion

The news media continue to play a key role in society by holding businesses and organizations to account for problems and situations that occur. Developing effective relationships with them is still an essential part of communication work. It means first knowing who they are and what they are interested in; this may be a geographic area or a specific subject. Remember to consider all relevant news media. Being able to reach all communities and be inclusive in the communication responses is critical to effectively managing everyday problems. There are databases and systems that can be introduced to support the communication and make it easier to identify the required media outlets you may want to work with. It is also important for all businesses to be aware of, and ready to respond to, international media interest in a situation. Even if the business does not operate internationally there is the possibility that a story will gain interest around the world that will draw further media queries.

Where possible work with the media rather than against them. This means investing time in understanding the media and how they operate. Spend some time in newsrooms to see what happens and the aspects and angles of stories that will increase media interest. Alongside this, help media organizations to know the business, how it works, who the key people are, and what it wants to achieve. Building these relationships will be important for future communication plans as well as developing responses to emerging problems. Remember to correct inaccuracies and work positively to try to overcome any challenging situations. Legal action can be taken as a last resort in dealing with a problem with a media organization.

Be clear about the approach that is being taken with the news media and at what point it may change or develop further. Each of the three tactics that have been highlighted brings challenges that need to be addressed, whether it is moving quickly to say something, or ensuring accurate information is available before speaking. Know what is required from each of the approaches and build it into an effective communication response plan. The news media is one element and does not operate alone. It is now more than ever interconnected with social media as all organizations have an online presence that helps to drive their newsgathering agenda. Social media is about more than online news, however, and this will be considered in the next chapter.

Notes

1 News Media Association website, History of Newspapers, www.newsmediauk. org/history-of-british-newspapers (archived at https://perma.cc/9RPC-JXWU)

2 Clarke, M (2012) *Digital Revolution*, Academic and Professional Publishing, www.sciencedirect.com/topics/psychology/digital-revolution (archived at https://perma.cc/HE2S-55HJ)

3 Washington Post (2022) [TikTok] www.tiktok.com/@washingtonpost?lang=en (archived at https://perma.cc/3EQV-3PXW)

4 Tobbit, C (2020) UK local newspaper closures: At least 265 titles gone since 2005, but pace of decline has slowed, *Press Gazette*, 20 August, www.pressgazette.co.uk/uk-local-newspaper-closures-at-least-265-local-newspaper-titles-gone-since-2005-but-pace-of-decline-has-slowed/ (archived at https://perma.cc/2XVR-UWEZ)

5 Turvill, W (2022) US newspaper circulations: Top 25 titles lost 30% of sales in two years, *Press Gazette*, 11 February, www.pressgazette.co.uk/us-newspaper-circulations/ (archived at https://perma.cc/5G9Y-TQ6Q)

6 International Public Relations Association website, www.ipra.org (archived at https://perma.cc/5EKK-G3UZ)

7 Davies, C (2021) McDonald's runs out of milkshakes amid 'supply chain issues', *Guardian*, 24 August, www.theguardian.com/business/2021/aug/24/mcdonalds-runs-out-of-milkshakes-due-to-supply-chain-issues (archived at https://perma.cc/Z4FH-FYKX)

8 Reuters (2021) McDonald's milkshakes off the British menu after supply chain issues, *Reuters*, 24 August, www.reuters.com/world/uk/mcdonalds-milkshakes-off-british-menu-after-supply-chain-issues-2021-08-24/ (archived at https://perma.cc/4DDH-SRC4)

9 Gruffydd, M (2021) 'We are experiencing issues': Costa Coffee is latest company with missing menu items, *Daily Express*, 26 August, www.express.co.uk/life-style/food/1482267/costa-coffee-missing-menu-items-food-drink-shortages-uk-lates (archived at https://perma.cc/N5GL-5VE3)

6

Managing social media

Introduction

The advent of social media was the moment of one of the biggest changes to modern-day communication. Gone were the days when the only form of mass communication was the news media. Since social networks came into existence, they have ensured that everyone can become a reporter and publisher sharing news, information and updates. It brought people together across continents in a way that had not been possible before. Broadcasting tools that make the creation of content easier have also grown. The changes have transformed the work of communicators and while traditional PR activities are still important, social media management has become a priority. Effective use of social media is a role in itself, with specialists working in this area and dedicated training courses available. All of this has happened in a short space of time.

Social media platforms started to emerge around the year 2000. The most notable moment was in 2004 when MySpace reached a million monthly active users.[1] Since then some of the early platforms have disappeared but there is now a selection of global networks that play a significant role in many people's lives. Facebook and YouTube both arrived in early 2000 and within a decade each had more than a billion users.[2] More than 3.6 billion people were using social media networks in 2020 and figures projected this would rise to almost 4.41 billion by 2025.[3] This means global social media usage was at 49 per cent in 2020.[4] This is a significant number and as access to technology continues to improve it will increase further. For communicators looking at the management of issues and incidents, social media has become increasingly central.

It is now the place where problems are first likely to be discussed, shared or commented upon. Issues will emerge through social media posts either directed at an organization or just shared with others. People will use it to raise customer complaints and will expect the business to respond in some way and to do so quickly. People will talk about bad service and will praise businesses that get things right. People will turn to social media to find news, information, and to read other people's views of brands and businesses. This makes the monitoring of social media and the ability to quickly respond a crucial part of any organization's communication mix. Social media should not be seen as just a case of managing a group of channels; it is about much more. It is about listening to what is being said, having direct conversations with customers and developing content to promote your products and services. Ultimately it is a way to build confidence in the business. For all the positive opportunities that social media has brought, however, there are as many problems and challenges. Some of these will be considered in this chapter, including looking at issues such as trolling, fake reviews and misinformation.

Networks and issues management

All businesses and organizations should have carefully considered and constructed social media strategies. Such strategies will detail how the business views social networks, the purpose of the channels it uses, and how it will respond to issues on social media. This strategy, as well as a possible critical incident plan, should detail how social media will be used to manage problems and issues. For the most serious situations, such as crises or emergencies, the communication strategy must include a detailed explanation of how social media will be used. It is not enough to have one line that says 'use social media'. It needs to cover in detail monitoring, information sharing, and management of misinformation. Each of these will be considered in this chapter and should assist in reviewing crisis communication approaches to social media.

Before developing the plan, it is vital to understand social media, social networks and which one can be used to manage emerging problems. Communicators need to be aware of the conventions that exist within different networks and the data around who is using which network and how. This information and data will change and develop so plans should be regularly reviewed and updated. There are many books available that consider social media and social media management for communicators. It is recommended that communicators use these to expand their knowledge and understanding of this aspect of work. Social media is important to issues management and it must also connect closely to the media management that was outlined in Chapter 5, through stakeholder management and with other aspects of communication. While plans about the use of social media are important, so too is making it work as part of a holistic approach to communication.

There are a number of ways that social networks can be used to support issues and incident management;

- monitoring for problems
- assessing emerging trends
- providing transparency
- accessing views
- managing the reputation of the business
- undertaking customer services work
- communicating directly with customers
- gathering support

Monitoring for problems

There are billions of users of social media and every day they are able to post comments, views, thoughts or updates on networks. Being able to identify a problem is critical and it starts with being able to find issues quickly on social media to then develop an appropriate intervention. Systems to monitor social media need to be in place. There are many ways technology can provide this ongoing monitoring support, but you can also seek to use social media staff and experts. Put a system in place that will give the business the most cost-effective way of monitoring social media. Communicators can support this monitoring by being aware of the business risks, ongoing problems, and previous issues and incidents. All that information will assist in trawling social media to find the posts that may be potentially critical or damaging to the business. It will provide parameters for the monitoring to consider and allow the monitoring to be more targeted.

Assessing emerging trends

Managing issues and incidents is not just about those things that happen to, or are caused by, the business itself. Events outside the business, within the industry, in a geographic area or in another company can have an impact on the reputation of the organization. Social media can be used to track emerging trends, threats and issues that may become a problem to the business and its sector. For example, in late 2012 the Food Safety Authority of Ireland tested a range of supermarket frozen beefburgers and ready meals and found horse DNA in more than a third of the samples. This quickly developed, with concerns about other products.[5] It demonstrates how an issue in one area can become a problem for other businesses. Being able to identify these emerging issues and trends in what is being posted on social media can provide information to allow a response to be developed ready for use when needed.

Providing transparency

Proactively using social media allows a business to give people an insight into the organization and how it operates. This can be the foundation of developing trust through connecting and sharing using the networks. When organizations invest in social media they can increase brand loyalty, offer special insight, and build a level of support. In the good times when there are no problems or issues being managed, this work can create a swell of support to utilize when something emerges. Being open and transparent can ensure there is back-up and support to call upon when needed.

Accessing views

For brands and organizations, social media allows anyone to gauge the views of groups including supporters, customers, and those with an issue in relation to the business. If it is monitored and used effectively it can be a great way to listen to what people's views are both about the business and any issues it is managing. It offers a window on what people are thinking. Even if the business is not tagged in the post, through effective monitoring it is simple to find what people are saying, where they are saying it, and what it means for the business.

Managing the reputation of the business

People will often use social media to raise issues about a business, which means a detailed knowledge of the channels can help identify these problems. Ultimately it supports reputation management. There is a chance to see issues early and hopefully before they grow and develop. Swift connections can be made to those posting about issues and this can be done both publicly and privately. The organization can ensure that the responses that are made support the brand position and present the image that is required.

Undertaking customer service work

The direct feedback that has been mentioned in the point above also opens the way for a business to manage customer service complaints online. Customers are able to speak directly to organizations through the social channels they use, and this means businesses need to be ready to pick up complaints made this way. If customer service activity sits outside the communication function, then it is vital they are brought together when looking at the best use of social media. Get it right here and an issue can be neutralized. Responses can be made to complaints in a public way which means others viewing will know that something has been done. It is why, even if the discussion is taken offline, it is essential to have given a reply publicly as well.

Communicating directly with customers

Before the advent of social media, the only ways to contact customers were through direct mailing and media advertising. The networks now mean that businesses can put their message, comment or news update out into the world without any form of censoring or editing. Customers have a chance to connect with brands they use, and this provides an opportunity to start a conversation and work on building trust. It also allows brands to test out developments within the business with their social media followers to gather views before they make any changes.

Gathering support

Ultimately, building a network on social media, proactively sharing information, and being seen to respond quickly to issues and complaints can build support. Even if they are not customers or users of the product or service, the responsive use of social media and effectively sharing and replying can boost reputation. When a problem does emerge there is a group on social media who can be vocal in support of the business and challenge views. Third-party support from individuals, customers and stakeholders who respond to issues and problems assists in issues management. This allows the business to take a back seat and wait until they feel compelled to step in and say something. As the network develops, they may be able to challenge views and address inaccuracies without the business having to step in at all. This can effectively provide extra resources to help an organization when dealing with an issue or problem.

Social media management can take significant resources away from other communication tasks when managing an emerging problem.

The scale of social media means that discussions can grow and escalate quickly, and additional specialist resources will be needed to step in and offer support to the existing team. Considering how to effectively manage day-to-day incidents means understanding the resources that are available, where additional support can be found, and the approach that will be taken to online commentary. It is essential for the organization to consider the skills and resources that are available in-house and how they may be supplemented when under pressure, as well as what technology is available. Many organizations face additional challenges when managing issues because they have blocked access to networks or have placed restrictions on the technology that can be used. If these things have been tackled ahead of any problems arising, it will put the organization in a stronger position when using social media.

Building a network

While social media has given a direct line to individuals and provided an opportunity for businesses to build networks of support, it has also given a voice to those who want to cause problems. Not everyone uses social media in an ethical and responsible way. People can post fake news or reviews about a business and its services. They can get involved in trolling a business, its leaders and even its employees. They can take direct action and build support to impact on the way a business operates. Careful consideration of social media within the management of everyday problems is needed. A social media strategy is needed, as mentioned before. People must know what they are doing with social media and why they are doing it. This strategy should be developed with the help of staff including those outside the communication function. It should be tested to ensure that it does what is needed and provides guidance that will inform decision making, particularly when dealing with an issue.

The work to develop social media use within a business must be done as part of the day-to-day communication and PR activity. If it is not in place, then there will be little time to do the groundwork needed to create an online presence when a problem occurs. When considering the approach to take using social media, ensure you have a background knowledge of the business and its relationship with social media. Be clear what social channels are used, how they are used, and who has access to use and update them on behalf of the organization. The brand on social media should reflect the brand that exists offline. Consider how the organization is currently using social media and review what it says about the business. Does it support the brand identity that exists? What principles are in operation to manage social media?

Then review how this can inform the response taken to issues and incidents. Consider the following questions:

- Will you respond publicly to any issues that are raised?
- Will you take the discussion offline?
- Will you use third parties to add support, share or post?
- How will you resource social media when under pressure?

In considering the approach to social media, remember that it is not possible to totally control what happens. People will post on their own pages, will make comments – accurate or not – and will share their views about situations. There is a limit to what organizations can do to directly address points of concern. Consider the sphere of influence that the business has and what this means to tackling problematic posts. At the heart of the circle the business has total control over what it posts and shares on social media. After that there are certain accounts, themes or individuals that the business may be able to influence. For example, a local councillor covering an area where the business is based may be willing to share information that the business posts. This can amplify the message. Another example would be where there is an account that provides comments, advice or news about the subject matter that is under the spotlight. This account may be interested in covering the issue and sharing the business response to the situation. Beyond this there are many accounts, comments and posts on social media that the organization has no control over. There are complaint mechanisms that are in place for social networks and these can be used, and if necessary legal redress can be considered. But there is a lot that falls outside these constraints. The approach needs to look at what action can be taken to marginalize the commentary or manage the situation and move towards the best outcome.

TOP TIP

Be clear with senior leaders and those at the top of the business that negative social media commentary cannot just be switched off or deleted. Managing expectations when dealing with an issue that is being spoken about on social media is essential. A lack of understanding may mean people at the top of the business think online problems can be erased. Educating senior leaders about social media will assist when the business is under pressure.

Having a risk management process in place to support the use of social media can help when looking at what interventions are required to deal with an emerging problem. The process will detail how the organization responds to social media issues and complaints. It will look at what information is needed to decide on the right course of action to take, when to respond, what sentiments will be noted but not replied to, and who is involved with providing the response. A simple flowchart can be created that will assist in the decision-making process (see Figure 6.1). It will look at what groups of situations may occur and what approach could be taken. Once a flowchart is developed and a risk management plan is outlined, it will be easier to secure support and agreement from senior managers when problems occur. It gives the communicator some freedom to operate without having to go through lengthy systems to have an approach authorized by those at the top of the business.

FIGURE 6.1   Example of a decision-making flowchart

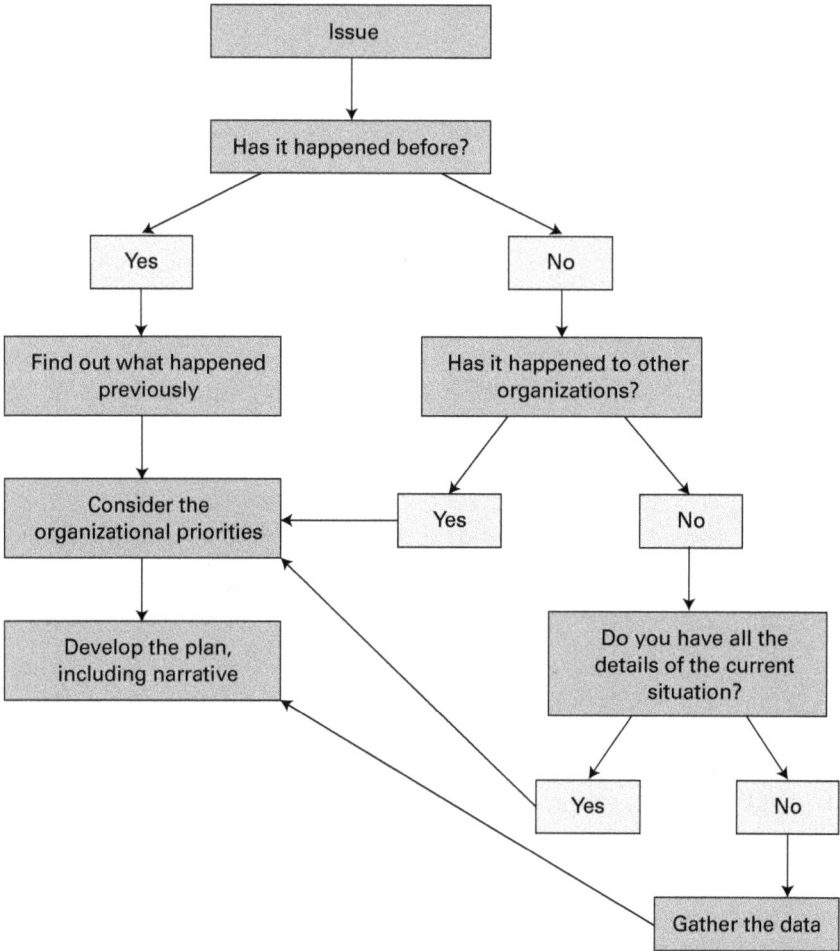

Monitoring social media

In managing everyday problems, the way social media is monitored is critical. Ensure systems are in place that provide an early alert of a challenging situation. The process should also detail how the information gathered from monitoring will be shared within the business, either with just the communication team or with other key departments such as customer service. It is essential to understand what risks exist, problems that may occur, and key elements that will form the basis of the monitoring. For example, always monitor for mentions of the company name and other key details such as the CEO's name, details of products and services, and key business buildings and locations. Look at what is important to the business and make it the focus of the monitoring that is taking place.

If you are unclear how to start this work, consider making a list of all the key words for the business including names, titles and locations, and put them at the heart of monitoring for comments. Should other departments be monitoring social media, such as customer services teams, then compare and discuss the monitoring list they use. Also review the system they have in place and see how it operates and links with any communication-led monitoring. There needs to be consistency across the way social media is used in different teams. If customer services deal with a query in a different way to the communication team it will impact on the confidence of customers. There are both free and paid-for monitoring systems that can be accessed, which means options are available to all organizations. Look at what is needed, what funding is available, and find a product or service that works within the resources available.

Keep a close watch for any spoof accounts that may be created that attempt to replicate the business. Be aware if there is branding used that gives the impression it is an official account, with the potential of a copyright breach. Both of these elements give grounds to report an account to the social media provider as being inappropriate. When a problem emerges it is possible that unhappy individuals may take direct action, which could include creating a spoof account, or one that is established solely to speak out against the business. Other action could include fake reviews that may appear on the company's website, on review sites or within Google. It is better to approach comments and posts assuming they are accurate before then checking their provenance rather than to automatically categorize them as fake. Taking a confrontational stance can enflame situations or lead to further criticism from those with a genuine issue.

> **TOP TIP**
>
> Keep a regular check on key sites where customers or individuals may leave reviews. Entries on sites such as Wikipedia and Google Reviews should be checked weekly to identify if there are any complaints or potentially fake reviews. They may be an indication of a problem that is emerging or highlight fake and negative sentiment. Developing a response to the fake reviews may include reporting them, correcting them, or presenting accurate information.

Monitoring social media can be a vast undertaking so focus on where most conversations and commentary are happening. Be clear what posts are linked to news media sites and coverage and what is from the public. Some accounts may be closed, such as Facebook Groups, but these can provide important insights into emerging problems and views. For example, residents' association Facebook groups covering a geographic area will include discussions about local public services and may be a place where a business is targeted. If there are ways to access them legitimately then build it into your social media plan. However, it may require the business to rely on third parties who act as the eyes and ears of the organization and highlight issues. Understanding customers and audiences is essential wherever they may be. Where will those people go when they have a complaint? What social networks are most popular with customers? Are there key accounts that they follow or access? Use this data and information to prioritize your monitoring activity.

Whenever an issue or incident has been managed it is important to reflect on what happened and add details that may be relevant to all monitoring systems. Consider what impact it had, what aspects of the communication plan brought results, and details of any lasting concerns from the issue. The details can help in the future identification of problems and keeping on top of the monitoring that is required. There may be a particular phrase that has been used, a hashtag that people introduced, or sentiment that emerged. All these need to be monitored to recognize any re-emergence of the issue itself or a related problem. Reflecting on events does not need to include a formal debrief but can simply be a moment to reflect and note key information. The details can then inform proactive and reactive communication, incident management, and support scenario planning to manage future incidents.

Using the data

Social media gives organizations access to a huge amount of data. Remember that this is only part of the discussion that will be taking place as a lot will be happening offline. As social media has grown, so has the ability for systems to harvest data from it which can then be used to support the development of both communication and the wider business. This is not the same as conducting social media monitoring. The data and insights that are gathered should be used at the start of planning for a communication campaign, action or initiative. It can also be used in the early stages of understanding an emerging issue. When the detail of the situation is understood you can look at what the data on social media says about it. What is it that people are concerned about? What action do they expect or want to see? Is the view of the business negative or neutral at this stage? Is any blame being attached? Gathering this information can be done through social media software, or a social media analyst could be engaged to undertake the work. Use the data to inform your communication approach and plans. If the situation continues to develop then look at re-running the data at key points during the management of the issue.

Data journalists are now in place within many media organizations and spend all their working day looking at what the statistics and information show about issues, incidents and situations. They may also be the people who uncover a set of circumstances that develop to become an issue the business has to manage. For example, if you have launched a product and the feedback has been negative, a data journalist may be able to highlight points to demonstrate this position and provide tangible statistics to underpin the story. This again highlights the importance of being ready and aware to recognize and respond to issues and incidents that may develop through social media. Understanding data, figures and statistics is an essential skill for all PR and communication professionals and should not be overlooked in any development plan.

Misuse and misinformation

There are many challenges when using social media, including misinformation, fake reviews and trolling. The misuse of social networks will always exist in some form while it is open to all with few restrictions. The main ways problems can occur on social media are negative posts, criticisms in online reviews, trolling of individuals, deliberate sharing of misinformation, and creating an angry online mob. What matters is that an organization is ready and able to respond to such situations and has plans in place for decision making. There are five questions to answer when looking at what may be potentially misinformation linked to the business circulating on social media.

1. Is it inaccurate or misleading?

If the post or comment is inaccurate then consider how you may be able to provide the correct information. If it is misleading, what could you say to present an accurate picture of what has happened? If the comment is legitimate criticism or personal opinion and this is obvious then it may not be appropriate to directly challenge it. For example, a vegan could dislike a meat production company and post that they dislike the company. This is a personal view and provided it does not go further is not misleading. However, if the same vegan made claims about how the meat production company operated that were inaccurate then it is appropriate to correct what has been said.

2. Is it illegal?

If a social media post has made some exaggerated claims that may be libellous and previous attempts to correct have been fruitless, it may be appropriate to seek legal advice. Taking legal action can be costly but if the damage to the business and its reputation is significant then such action is essential. The post and account should be reported to the social media provider as they may also be able to act. This may mean the suspension of an account. But remember that even though an account is suspended people can still quickly establish a new profile and continue to make the claims. This can become like a game of cat and mouse where the business is in a never-ending race to stop the individual.

3. Does it contravene the network's usage policies?

Even if the post is not illegal it may still breach the policies that are in place for the social media channel. Review what restrictions apply to each of the networks that the business operates on. Understand the scenarios where accounts and individuals can be reported and the circumstances that need to be in place. For example, an account that targets employees of a business may be found to be harassing individuals and contravene the policies of the social network. In such cases systems exist that will allow people to report concerns.

4. Could it substantially damage the business?

If the account criticizing the business has no followers, comments only a couple of times, and is not very active then the comments may have insignificant impact. Being aware of the comments is important but no further action may be needed beyond monitoring for future developments. If, however, the comments are having, or could have, a significant impact then action and a planned response are required. This response may be directly or indirectly through the network, or face to face if there is a need to take things offline. It is important to ensure there is clarity about the situation, and to act if reputation is seriously compromised.

5. Do you need to respond?

Having considered the first four questions, ask then whether it is important to provide a response to the situation. If deciding not to act at this stage, then look at how you can monitor for changes. But if it has become important to provide some form of response to protect the reputation of the business then put a clear plan in place which will allow the organization to correct misinformation.

There is no simple algorithm that will review and consider what action should be taken. Instead, it is important to assess all the information you have, look at what others have done, and consider what impact there has been. Communicators need to develop systems and processes that will support them in addressing concerns on social media, but also need to train themselves in risk identification.

Dealing with a negative social media post will depend on how risky it is to the business, whether as mentioned above it is illegal or is inappropriate according to the network's policy. In low-level cases monitoring what happens may be the most appropriate course of action. It may be a lone voice commenting about a subject few people are interested in. Remember the first step is to verify whether the comments are justified, whether they are inaccurate, and if they come from a legitimate account. It may be appropriate to make a direct connection with the person posting on social media. Remember to review the 10 interventions guide in Chapter 4. As mentioned, negative reviews can also be a huge challenge to an organization and monitoring for problems is important. The post may be a one-off or could be part of consistent action from groups or individuals. Again, if the commentary is accurate then it may be appropriate to apologize and state what is happening to rectify the situation.

Always avoid starting arguments on social media and demonstrate that the business is attempting to be reasonable in responding. Arguments and disagreements publicly on social media involving a business or brand look unprofessional. The handling of the dispute will become as much of a potential story as the issue being debated. If the review is unexpected and there are suspicions it may be fake, then look at how you can legitimately drown it out with positive reviews from genuine customers. It is important to do this in an ethical way.

IN FOCUS

A good example of how to approach negativity and criticism can be seen in the actions of the Hampshire and Isle of Wight Air Ambulance in November 2021. A complaint they had received stated: 'Can you explain when you decided to fly at 1750ft from St Mary's Hospital to Southampton General Hospital at 4 am over residential properties – waking occupants. Inconsiderate I think, will NO longer be donating to your cause.' The communication team decided to take a calculated risk and share a redacted version without the individual's details to give them an opportunity to respond publicly. Their reply was: 'We always try our best to be there for the people of Hampshire and the Isle of Wight, but messages like this really affect our team's morale. We are sorry the helicopter wakes people up at night, but it is not our intention to disrupt your evening, but rather save someone's life.' The post received 2.5 million impressions on Twitter as well as local and national news media coverage. It also led to thousands of pounds being given in donations to the Air Ambulance, according to the Director of Marketing and Communications.[6] The risk paid off and demonstrated how people can be united to support a worthy cause.

Trolling is when insulting and abusive messages are posted on social media in an attempt to annoy or upset someone. They may be a one-off where there is just one post and this is not followed up by anything further. While these can be upsetting, they are less problematic than continuous campaigns targeting an individual. If trolling affects an employee, then the business has a duty of care to that member of staff. They need to look at ways to protect them from online harm, particularly when the abuse is linked to the work they do. The simplest approach is to mute, block or ban the troll from posting on the social media account. Business accounts can do this; however, it can become a story in its own right when news media assess who is blocked or banned from sites. But for individuals it can provide a welcome break from the negative posts that they are being targeted with.

Organizations may be able to rotate staff on social media so that they do not face relentless targeting by trolls. In addition, inappropriate posts by the troll can be reported to the social network provider. But there are occasions when being positive, approaching the situation with humour or refusing to engage with the troll can address the situation. Trolls want to make an impact and can thrive by getting continued responses to their posts. Each situation needs to be assessed for what is happening, who is involved, and what impact their actions have had or are having. Plans can be developed based on that information and with the feedback of the person being trolled.

Social media can allow people to gather together and be united in opposition to someone, something or some development. Within a short space of time there can be a group created to challenge or criticize an organization. An example is the creation of the 'I Hate Ryanair' website and social media accounts. Many other organizations have faced similar 'anti' groups. This crowdsourcing using social media has been able to galvanize individuals into action including making complaints, creating online petitions and demanding changes. This ability to bring people together is also a big opportunity for communicators. Everyday communication activity on social media can work to build a network of supporters who can be activated to assist the business when dealing with an issue or incident. It is why understanding your customers, audiences and others is so critical to daily business. If an organization knows who they are, where they are and what they want from the business the proactive communication can satisfy requirements. In turn it builds trust and confidence which can help create that network of support.

CASE STUDY

What happened?

Trolling is increasingly a problem for organizations as spokespeople and those in the public eye become targeted. TV presenter Naga Munchetty spoke about her approach to the online abuse she faced in November 2021. She spoke about not caring about the comments, which defiantly demonstrated the trolls were having no effect. On her Twitter account, Ms Munchetty will reply to comments and call them out. In many cases the original post by the troll will be deleted once it had been challenged.[7] It demonstrates how a direct approach may not stop the comments, but it diminishes their importance and prevents problems from developing.

However, trolling can become serious and lead to threats to the individual being targeted. In a case from October 2021, the head of Hospitality Ulster, Colin Neill, spoke about the need to increase security at his home following abuse on social media.[8] Mr Neill had been in the media to represent the hospitality industry talking about the impact of the Covid-19 pandemic restrictions on the sector. He also spoke of concerns that more staff may become the target of trolls. This highlights the need to have clear social media strategies in place and systems to identify problems and then take action to protect employees from abuse.

In a third case, in December 2021 a restauranteur from Blackpool, England, turned detective to find a troll who had been leaving fake reviews. Steven Hoddy brought a civil case against the individual, saying that fake reviews can ruin businesses. The 'troll' was ordered to pay £6,000 in costs for 'spreading malicious falsehoods'. Mr Hoddy's initial response to the first review was to make a sarcastic remark and the post was removed. But a further eight reviews were made by different accounts that were able to be connected to the same person. Mr Hoddy said that fake reviews damaged businesses and those posting needed to be able to justify what they were posting. He called for the law to be changed to make it easier to identify who has left review posts.[9] In challenging the review he was able to demonstrate it was bogus and the action gave him a platform to correct perceptions of the business.

KEY LEARNING POINTS

- Social media presents opportunities for all, from the troll through to the business and its communication team.

- Have a plan for how you will respond to negative comments online, to fake reviews and to trolling. Use it to inform the intervention that you put in place.

- Anyone can become the target of online abuse, from the CEO through to employees on the frontline. Businesses can also be targeted through misinformation. It is important to identify these problems so that prompt action can be taken.

- The sphere of influence that the business has will be limited and it is not always possible to remove negative social media posts. But as seen with the case studies, often a challenge back to the person posting can lead to it being deleted.

- Online abuse and challenges do not have to be accepted. Feedback that is genuine can help a business to develop or to address a problem, but if the feedback is fake, it can threaten the business and its reputation so should be addressed, particularly if legal action needs to be considered.

Conclusion

In tackling everyday problems and issues social media has a critical position both as an opportunity and as a threat. Whatever the organization and those at the top think of social media it is something that must be considered, planned for and engaged with to be effective in managing issues. The communicator needs to have the relevant skills and knowledge to be able to advise on how to approach social media use and educate those at the top of the business. The best way to manage this is to have a social media strategy and a plan in place for when and how to use social media in incident response.

All this is only possible if there are robust monitoring systems and processes in place to alert the communication team to emerging issues. Posts that include negative comments about the business need to be identified so they can be considered. If the feedback is accurate, it can highlight a potential problem area and allow swift action to be taken to address the issue. If it is a fake comment or misinformation, then it should be corrected and challenged to limit the possible impact on the organization's reputation. Having a flowchart of what action could be taken in certain circumstances will assist in developing the intervention to be made. It can also give the communicator the freedom to move quickly to address situations without requiring authorization, which may create delays. To do this the approach and flowchart will need to have been seen and signed off by those at the top of the business.

Despite all the challenges, the negativity, the trolls and the potential impact on reputation from social media it still presents huge opportunities for the communicator looking to effectively manage everyday problems. It allows the business to identify issues at an early stage, to garner support for their position, to open up to its followers, and to build online networks. Social media gives the business the opportunity to get their message out quickly to key groups and individuals without editing, and then monitor the feedback. All this information can help in making decisions about the next steps to take to manage the emerging issue. Developing the appropriate communication intervention to an emerging problem needs all relevant information to be considered. The next chapter looks at how to make decisions more effectively when under pressure.

Notes

1 Ortiz-Ospina, E (2019) The rise of social media, *Our World in Data*, www.ourworldindata.org/rise-of-social-media (archived at https://perma.cc/ZE7T-W4G8)

2 Ibid.

3 Statista (2022) Number of social media users worldwide 2017 to 2025, www.statista.com/statistics/278414/number-of-worldwide-social-network-users/ (archived at https://perma.cc/BA4K-Q6CT)

4 Ibid.

5 Lawrence, F (2013) Horsemeat scandal: the essential guide, *Guardian*, 15 February, www.theguardian.com/uk/2013/feb/15/horsemeat-scandal-the-essential-guide (archived at https://perma.cc/LC85-Z4AJ)

6 Wilson, K (2021) On Saturday, my marketing team asked if they could take a calculated risk [LinkedIn] 29 November, https://www.linkedin.com/posts/keithwilsonpr_team-marketing-viralmarketing-activity-6871707272389636096-0f61 (archived at https://perma.cc/8RKU-NXWP)

7 Dean, C (2021) 'There are so many angry, unhappy people'; BBC's Naga Munchetty hits out at 'deeply miserable' trolls who called her 'ugly', *Guardian*, 9 November, www.dailymail.co.uk/tvshowbiz/article-10182125/BBCs-Naga-Munchetty-adresses-comments-deeply-miserable-trolls.html (archived at https://perma.cc/8SRC-U4C9)

8 BBC News Online (2021) Covid-19: Hospitality staff threatened over proof of Covid status, https://www.bbc.com/news/uk-northern-ireland-59554917 (archived at https://perma.cc/H2FG-G22Q)

9 BBC News Online (2021) TripAdvisor: Blackpool restauranteur turns detective to unmask 'troll', 15 December, www.bbc.co.uk/news/uk-england-lancashire-59655205 (archived at https://perma.cc/BCE5-H82P)

7

Effective decision making under pressure

Introduction

Managing everyday problems and issues relies on effective decision making taking place from the moment the situation is identified. But we rarely spend any time looking at how we make decisions, what may be affecting us, and whether we can improve how we approach looking at the options available. Even if plans are in place there is always room to improve and develop how we make judgements about what happens. Making decisions is not just something that affects those leading communication teams or in charge of the communication response. An effective response to manage issues and incidents requires everyone to feel competent and confident to make decisions. If all the decisions are made by one person, or a small group, it will quickly become a bottleneck to moving forward. But how do we ensure consistency in the approach? When is it right to challenge the agreed perspective on the situation? And how do we become aware of how our own views may impact on the path that we choose to take?

The starting point has to be to consider how decisions are currently made, both personally and within a team. Look at what steps you go through, even if they are instinctual, and run through what happens when faced with a decision that needs to be made. It may be easier to start by considering a decision that is based around an unimportant situation such as, what should I have for breakfast? When should I leave work? Assessing these everyday situations where choices are made will demonstrate what happens when planning the way forward. It may be that you make a random choice, or that you look at the information you have at hand and what that may mean to the decision, or you do what you have done before in a similar situation. You can take the same approach for considering decision making at work, even if it is a complex and challenging situation.

Why is effective decision making important?

In managing a situation, it is crucial not to only rely on a gut feeling about what is the best option to take. Instinctual decision making is open to lots of problems, including a failure to see the broader picture, internal biases, and an attempt to follow previous steps regardless of any changes in the circumstances. There have been many commentators and educators who have argued from both sides: that gut feelings cannot be trusted, and that we should listen to them. What is clear is that you need to understand feelings and beliefs that you hold and be clear about who and what you are trusting. Previous chapters have looked at the strategies that can be employed, the channels that can be used, and the messages to put in place, but to manage situations the communicator needs to be able to make the right decisions in these and other areas. This makes decision making a fundamental part of managing issues and incidents.

Having a clear head and a way to keep focused on what matters when considering the developing situation and what to do is essential. This can become more challenging when there are time pressures and a need to operate at speed. Decisions can be made quickly to meet a deadline, to satisfy a demand, or to try to move forward at speed. When they are made quickly there are more opportunities for errors and for key information to be overlooked. Any problem that emerges will require many decisions to be taken and they need to be the right decisions at the right times. Developing an approach to decision making or a system that will assist you in making choices increases the possibility of a successful outcome. It will also give a framework that can be used when people are under pressure and may be struggling to decide what to do next.

Working to a system for decision making will:

- support a better response
- enable the communicator to be more effective
- allow for fewer surprise developments, and
- avoid things developing unexpectedly

Improved management of situations can arise when thinking through how to make key decisions rather than just blundering forward and hoping for the best outcome. Recognize that there are rarely just two options but a range of decisions that can be taken. There will be a significant amount of information available, usually some gaps in understanding the developing situation, and a range of options that could be taken to manage the issue. For example, a business that has received an online complaint about a product, service or member of staff could ignore it, could respond publicly, could respond privately, could apologize, could check the validity of the comment, could share a feedback form – there are many other options. Being able to take the most effective step at the right point will save a business time, money and resources as well as prevent reputational damage.

There are four broad systems of decision making: rationality, bounded rationality, intuition and creative.[1] In the *rationality* approach you gather all the relevant information before considering it and deciding. However, it can lead to analysis paralysis where there is so much information it becomes confusing to identify the options and to make a decision. There is also a challenge that the first information and solution that is identified may become the favoured position without evidence to support it. The structure that this approach provides is helpful and the eight steps of decision making will be considered later in this chapter.

Bounded rationality is when the options are limited so that there is a manageable set of information to be considered. People will choose the best available alternative without having all the options in front of them. *Intuitive* decision making happens when decisions are made without having any conscious reasoning. People use their own experience and look for cues about previous patterns of decision making within the situation they face. *Creative* decision making is seen as a way to take organizations forward. People need to have expertise in an area before they set the problem aside and let their subconscious look at options, aiming for a 'eureka' moment. It is helpful to recognize the ways decisions are made with an aim of developing your approach through training to become more effective with decision making. This assists us in identifying the pitfalls of the approaches that may be considered.

Steps in decision making

In a rational approach to decision making there are eight steps for dealing with an emerging problem or issue. Understanding the steps can help you to navigate the way forward and to decide on a solution and course of action. Working through these stages when there is time and no pressure to develop a speedy response will help in preparing to deal with problems. There is no time limit on how long to take on each of the sections and it will depend upon the circumstances that are being considered:

1 **See the need to decide**
   The starting point is the identification of a decision being required. In the case of looking at managing an issue or incident this will follow shortly after the issue emerges. The early actions will require decisions to be made as a plan is developed.

2 **Consider the circumstances**
   Before looking into the specifics of what the situation is and what is known about it, look at the environment at the time. Consider what events are taking place in the world, what is in the media, and what are the trends that are being highlighted. This information will assist in providing a context to what is taking place.

3 Research information

Identify the information, data and insight that is required to support the decision making. Researching the situation in as much detail as possible to present the options that may be available.

4 Look at options for solutions

Using the information that you have available both from Step 2 looking at external factors and Step 3 gathering information and data, consider the options that could be taken to deal with the issue. In the management of an emerging critical issue this provides the possible actions within the response plan.

5 Evaluate the options

Once a list of the possible approaches and options has been created then look at the positive and negative elements linked to each of them. This needs a calm head and the ability to be aware of the things that affect our judgements. Biases that we hold can influence the approach we take.

6 Decide on the next steps

Making the decision and setting out the way forward is not the end of the process. It sets out actions to take and may also consider further decisions and actions that may follow if the situation develops.

7 Implement

It is now time to put the decision into practice and follow through on the actions that have been outlined. If additional support, resources or staffing are required then they need to be in place to ensure that the decision is implemented effectively. Consider who needs to know about the decision. What action is going to be taken and how is it going to be put in place?

8 Review the situation

The final step is to review the situation and consider the impact of the decision that was made and implemented. The situation should be monitored to support this detailed understanding and, as detailed at Step 6, further actions or changes may be needed.

This can be considered as part of scenario planning, which looks at what may happen and the additional decisions that may emerge.

Running through these steps will help to prevent focusing just on intuitive decision making. It will also ensure the consequences of both the situation and the decisions that are made are considered. The process can limit the possibility of panic setting in, and speedy decisions being made that are not based on firm foundations of information. It can balance the conflict that can take place between what the head is saying is logical to do and what the heart is attached to emotionally. For effective issues management the two need to be blended, as understanding the emotional impact of the situation is important when considering the actions to take. It is also a key part of ensuring a sensitive and people-focused approach.

The eight steps did not include considering your own feelings and understanding any biases, but this is work that should take place before you start to make decisions. Previous chapters have detailed the importance of a diverse approach to managing issues and to understanding the position from which you are working. At the point of making a decision, be clear what you personally feel towards the situation, how that may make you feel and possibly act. It is important to understand the biases so that we can overcome the impact they may have on our decision making.

Judgements and biases

Judgements can be made in a number of ways but will be affected by the biases that we hold about the world around us. They are made with a combination of personal qualities, knowledge and experience that form opinions and affect decisions that are taken.[2] There is also an element of luck that can affect whether a decision leads to a successful outcome but the possibility of this can be reduced by building our ability to make judgements. Good judgements can be made by building our knowledge and experience while being aware of our biases.

Professor Sir Andrew Likierman has identified six aspects of judgement that are more likely to 'stack the cards in our favour'.[3] First, we need to check that we have actively heard and understood what has been said. Research shows that there are different abilities of taking information in from reading and listening. Second, can you trust the information that is being provided and who it is from? Third, consider what relevant information and experience you have. Things will change as the situation develops but it is important to accept what you know and what limitations there are. Fourth, ask how the beliefs and feelings you have may affect the choices that you make. Fifth, look at the options and who may need to be involved to improve decision making. Finally, consider whether the approach can be delivered. These aspects are linked to the eight steps of decision making that have been outlined.

Good judgement and decision making requires an understanding of the biases that may impact on what we do. Cognitive biases appeared as a term in the 1970s and details the systematic but potentially flawed patterns people have to respond to judgements and decision-making challenges.[4] There are many biases, and some common ones can have the most impact on decision making. They can also impact, as outlined above, on the judgements that are made:

- **Analogy**
  People use their own experience to decide what to do, and what action to take. This creates challenges if your experience cannot be replicated, if there are changeable external factors, or the previous decision making was flawed.

- **Availability**
  The latest information that we have or the first answer that presents itself is something we may be biased towards. Information that is available now will override any other details and if it is something we can recall then we afford it more importance.

- **Groupthink**
  Decisions may be influenced by comments and suggestions made by other people. This can be challenging for people working together in an organization as they may develop a shared way of

approaching situations. People want to 'fit in' and so put their own views aside to join the group.

- **Sunflower**
  Any decision making will be handed over to those in charge of a team, unit or organization. The individual is unwilling or unable to make a decision themselves. Instead, they push all decisions upwards and wait for the leader to give their view of the situation.

- **Overconfidence**
  In this situation people overestimate their abilities. They believe they are better equipped than others to make a decision. It can lead to decisions being made in isolation, without the full information that is available and without listening to a range of opinions. It can be damaging and is difficult to challenge among those in leadership positions.

- **Confirmation**[5]
  Decisions are made using information that supports the beliefs and opinions we currently hold. We search the information available to find those elements that reinforce our views, and anything that conflicts with that position will be ignored. It is like searching Google and taking the top search results that support our position without looking further.

Overcoming these biases is important if we are going to be able to consider the issues or problems that are emerging and define the appropriate way forward to manage them. One of the most critical elements is ensuring there is self-awareness and an understanding of how you think and act. There are steps that can be taken to manage biases including questioning your approach to the situation and opening up to the views of others. Use the eight steps of the decision-making process to ensure you are not letting biases affect your judgement. Where possible take a moment to step back and acknowledge that the decision may not be the right one. Consider what alternative options you have thought about and check how objective your decision making is.

TOP TIP

Take some time to consider how you make decisions and how the above biases may affect your thinking. Be aware of the beliefs and feelings that you have and recognize how they may sway you. Once this self-awareness is in place you can then take steps to manage or eradicate them.

Managing biases

Self-awareness is a key way to try to manage the biases that impact on our lives and decision making. It is not possible to completely remove them but there are ways to keep them in check or to recognize when they may be impacting on our approach to situations. Ask what you know about the situation and be clear where there are gaps in your understanding. Acknowledging the uncertainties is important to making decisions about the initial approach but also to planning for the potential scenarios that may develop. When faced with an emerging problem, be clear what you know about the position and try to understand the feelings that you may have to the situation. Then consider how you are going to plan forward. It is a moment to reflect on the eight steps of the decision-making process for support. But recognize when you may have some 'gut' responses to the situation. Look at whether they are linked to knowledge, experience or the biases that have been mentioned.

Be aware of how you may filter the information that you hear or read. Our beliefs and values can influence what we take from the details that we learn about an issue or situation. Check the understanding you have against what others know about the situation and identify when you may have focused on some elements and ignored others. Understand where you need to increase your knowledge and experience, and how you can develop a network of trusted advisers to assist you. Managing our biases is helped when we step outside our own perceptions and experiences and listen to others. In 1967 Peter F Drucker, in an article about effective decisions, said, 'Failure to go out and look is the typical reason for persisting in a course of action long after it has ceased to be appropriate or even rational.'[6] This highlights a key aspect of effective decision making, which is to look for information, to question the details, and to gather alternative perspectives on what has emerged.

Involving others in your decision making can help you challenge those biases that may appear. The way you gather views about a situation can be both formal and informal. Formal processes may already exist within an organization, such as customer panels and key stakeholder networks. Informal consultation may be taken by contacting employees or those outside the business to gather their views on an ad hoc basis. These networks can provide alternative views of the situation and the possible action to take and can support the research and information-gathering phase of the decision-making process. To be ready to respond to emerging situations it is important to consider what networks are available to consult with. If there are customer panels, focus groups or others, consider how you can work with them before a problem develops.

Discussions ahead of time will assist in planning and preparing to address issues and incidents. Consider working with such groups to scenario plan and test views on approaches and responses that you may make about the most likely situations. For example, test the plan for responding to social media criticism and gather the views of others about the narrative, actions, and escalation plan. The decisions made can be improved by gathering a broad range of information and considering alternative views. It is also possible to work with employees and internal stakeholders to gather views provided they feel supported to be open and honest.

Moving at speed

Making decisions when you have time and space is easier than attempting to do it at speed. When there are pressures to act because of deadlines, external demands or other elements, things are more challenging. This is when having a clear process to work to can help.

It provides a structure to support you as a situation emerges and requires swift attention. Consciously developing the use of a process in day-to-day work will help it to become imprinted into behaviour. When an issue emerges, the structure will be there to provide support. It is also available when there is pressure to act quickly to minimize the impact of an issue, to bring it to a conclusion or to respond, and can challenge effective decision making. Beyond having a process or system to use there are other ways to be ready to deal with such pressured situations. Preparation is key to being ready to address emerging issues and make necessary decisions.

A starting point is to understand the risks that an organization holds, and what previous problems have occurred. The next chapter will look at how to make better use of the learning from dealing with problematic issues. This is also helpful when developing approaches to tackling everyday issues. For each of these issues start by considering the scenarios that may occur and look at the responses that may be required. This can become a checklist of possible actions that can be taken depending on the circumstances of what is occurring. Developing simulations of situations can assist when working through what may happen and considering the communication that may be required. Simulations and exercises are often focused just on the major incident and crisis situation, but they can be used to prepare for issues and incident management. This will also support planning for future decisions and considering the level of complexity involved. Look at these possible situations and know what data, information and analytics may assist in decision making. Prepare by making sure the information is available, or you are aware of a quick route to access it. Building connections across the organization with stakeholders, customers and other key groups will support in speedy decision making. You will be able to contact the right person, quickly, and gather their vital feedback on the next steps and options available. Develop relationships with key people and make sure they understand how to assist the communication response to emerging issues.

Developing professional skills to manage situations, build resilience and improve our decision making are important in supporting operating at speed. Continuous learning and development should be in place for all communicators. It is a fundamental part of being prepared to deal with situations, particularly when they happen outside normal work areas or require a swift response. Never be afraid to ask for help from others. Decisions do not have to be made in isolation. Other people and their views can, and should, be involved when considering what to do. Take the time to speak to others and listen to what they say about the situation and the proposed way forward. If you have been working with a mentor or coach, they can assist in helping you to consider how to approach decision making and what may happen. And as mentioned earlier, consultation can be a key factor in effective decision making to address an emerging issue.

Decision-making flowchart

Having a flowchart can support decision making, particularly when under pressure, as it provides a simple system to work through. A sample flowchart can be seen in Chapter 6. Start with looking at whether you have all the available information about the issue. If you do then you can progress to the next phase. However, if you are concerned that data and insight may exist that has not been accessed then undertake further research before moving to the next stage. Next, consider whether the situation is stable and not getting worse at the moment. Again, if it is stable you can move to the next phase but if it is worsening then it is important to move to fast-track action. The fast-track route will look at what you know, who is affected, and what is being said before taking some form of communication action. If it is stable, then look at what is known about any past experience that may be similar. What happened, and what was the action taken and result from it? This information can help in identifying the implications of what is happening.

Consider the business and organizational priorities and what this means for the situation that has emerged. Is it going to undermine confidence in the business or is it a minor inconvenience to the work that is being done? If the priorities and values are impacted, then identify how they are affected and what it may mean for any action that is taken. If they are not affected then look at the media, social media and other commentary on the situation. At this point move to look at the options available to respond. However, if there is no media, social media or commentary on the situation then consider if it is because you do not have the relevant data – in which case return to the starting point and work through the flowchart again – or because there has not yet been any commentary on the situation. If it is the latter, then again move to look at the options that are available to act.

This simple approach can ensure that you are taking account of what is known at this stage, what further information may be required, and the impact of the information that is available. It is not anticipated that people will need to continue to rely upon a flowchart when they become more proficient in working through the information that they have. The flowchart shown in Chapter 6, Figure 6.1, is a basic outline supporting the eight steps of decision making; it can be developed to include links to individuals and departments that may be required to agree activities or sign off actions in relation to an emerging issue. Use it as a basis to build your own decision-making flowchart to manage emerging issues. It can benefit new members of the team or those who are brought in to work with communicators.

Triggers to further action

Effective decision making becomes critical when looking at how a problem or issue develops and the steps that may need to be taken. In Chapter 4 the principles of intervention were outlined, and these support the decisions that are required to identify the initial action. But as a problem may develop it is important to review the position and look at whether further action is necessary. Being able to recognize when to do more, or to do something differently, means understanding the detail about what is taking place, to review scenarios that may follow, and then be able to spot the triggers to further action. The trigger points will show the need to escalate the action that may have already been taken. The escalation plan can be created during the initial planning phase by looking at the developments that may take place. There are 10 triggers that should be considered for each incident when creating an escalation plan:

1 **An increase in social media commentary about the subject**
   When there is a growth in the online discussion of the situation it may require responses or further action. It is important to recognize the point at which more steps should be taken. This will vary due to a number of factors including the risks that the organization is prepared to carry, the amount of interest, and the voracity of the commentary.

2 **An increase in media reports on the subject**
   In the same way as social media commentary may lead to further action, so should a rise in media interest in the issue. If a team become aware of an increase in questions about the situation it may mean a move from reactive communication to proactive. Factors that need to be considered are the number of articles, the severity of any criticism or the potential for criticism, and the amount of subsequent interest from people.

3 **A move from local to national and possibly international coverage**
   Once the media are aware of the issue and are covering it, interest may spread. What started as a local news media story can be taken up by the national or even international media. The approach that is being taken should be reviewed and reconsidered as there will be further pressures on the organization caused by the widening of interest. As mentioned in Chapter 5 it will be important to understand how the international media work and consider what action may be needed specific to them.

4 **The problem itself is getting worse**
   Even if there is no media or social media coverage yet, if the situation itself is deteriorating it requires a review of the communication approach being taken. Further steps will need to

be taken to move to a proactive approach or to prepare for the inevitable increase in social media and news media interest. Assessing the information and using it to assist decision making is essential and the flowchart can support this.

5 **More people are being affected by the situation**
If the growth of the issue means that more people are both becoming aware of, and being affected by the situation then it is time to review the communication plan. This is a trigger to more interest from the news media, more social media commentary, and affected people coming together to ensure they have a louder voice to demand change, apology, recompense or other action from the business.

6 **People are joining together to comment/demand action about the issue**
As more people are affected there is more likelihood that they may come together as a protest group, campaign group or just a collection of affected people increasing their impact. If campaign groups are created the situation is rapidly deteriorating and decisive action is needed. The groups will be able to foster media coverage and will be vocal on social media.

7 **High-profile people and/or celebrities are affected by the situation**
When members of the public are affected it is a trigger, but if the people involved are well known, high profile or celebrities then it can have more impact. The personal stories of people that are in the media spotlight will travel far. It may require further communication action to be taken.

8 **Concern has been raised by stakeholders, shareholders or politicians**
If key groups and individuals are unhappy with the current position, the response, or how things are being managed then it is time to review what communication is taking place. Stakeholder engagement and public affairs are a critical part of all issue and incident management. Maintaining confidence among these key connections can boost the response.

9 There is influential commentary on the situation

When the situation sparks a statement or some words from someone in authority it can increase the pressure to demonstrate that action is being taken. The involvement of a political figure or business leader can escalate the issue and require a revision of the approach being taken. As mentioned in Chapter 1, some issues are politically driven or may be sustained because of political interests in what is happening.

10 The problem is continuing over a sustained period of time

The longer the issue continues without being resolved the more likelihood there is of scrutiny being increased. Even if the situation does not deteriorate, the fact that it is continuing will put pressure on the approach being taken. Some issues may exist for months or even years before something triggers an escalation and more communication activity.

There may be other triggers specific to the situation that is being managed so use the above list as a starting point to develop a bespoke plan. For each of the circumstances that may lead to an intensification of the situation consider what options you have and the actions that could be taken. The more trigger points are considered, and a comprehensive escalation plan created, the more proficient you will become in identifying changes that require the revision of communication activity.

Dealing with pressure

Issues can linger with organizations for some time, or a series of issues could hit a business in a short space of time, putting pressure on the communicators. The demands of the day job may be growing as the focus is on responding to the situation that is emerging. Whatever the impact is, building resilience is a key element of modern-day communication management. Being able to manage the pressure and find ways to continue to be calm and have a clear head for decision making is critical. Resilience is not about being strong but being able to bounce back when these stressors have been in place. If you are exhausted, frustrated, or rushing to act it can impact on the ability to make decisions. The position can become foggy, and a lack of clarity as seen earlier is problematic when looking at effective decision making. It is important to step back and view the situation and the information you have, recognizing where gaps in information may be, before considering the best approach and the escalation plan. Building resilience will help with achieving this and with the wellbeing and mental health of communicators.

How people deal with pressure will vary. The methods put in place to increase resilience need to work for individuals but there are a number of ways people can approach this. Have support mechanisms in place for managing both personal and professional life. These supportive contacts are people who can provide space to decompress from situations and to switch off. They may be friends, colleagues (although it is difficult to do this with those in a line management chain), mentors or coaches. Having a mentor or a coach is beneficial to all communicators regardless of their role and aspirations for the future. But find the right person who you can connect with. Mentoring and coaching relationships are usually for a fixed period of time to deal with specific issues or situations. They can also run over a longer period of time to support professional development.

The starting point to building personal resilience is developing self-awareness, similar to that mentioned in reviewing our judgements and biases. Being aware of the way pressure manifests itself in you both physically and psychologically will act as an early warning to developing problems. This allows action to be taken to prevent the pressure affecting wellbeing and to avoid becoming, or feeling, overwhelmed. At this point taking action is important. It may be a five-minute break to step away from the computer and the situation, a moment to practise breathing techniques, or time to regroup to get a perspective on the issue. If this is challenging, then have processes that can help and support by giving a step-by-step guide to achieve the required result. Plans and processes give a framework to support decision making. This can be particularly helpful when dealing with unfamiliar circumstances as it provides some certainty.

Professional development

Training can help with managing pressure and building resilience. Professional development is more than just expanding communication skills. Developing systems, plans and processes that support how you deal with situations can be taught. This may be through training courses, personal development plans, mentoring or coaching. Review your own resilience levels and ability to bounce back from problems or challenges. Issues can emerge at any point so having resilience can sustain you through the initial demands of developing the response and considering the future actions. When others may be angry, frustrated, confrontational or emotional, it is essential that the communicator can keep calm and have a cool head to keep things in proportion. Use data and insight to support communicating to senior managers or CEOs who may be annoyed with details of the emerging issue. Be aware of the possibility of groupthink affecting those connected with the incident and the response to it. Be ready to find ways to step away and regain the perspective that is required and bring back a valued external view of what is developing. As mentioned earlier, external consultation and involvement of other voices can support this.

One way to review the approach, biases and ability to react is to test the response to issues and incidents. Tests and exercises are not just for crisis communication and training, they can be introduced to assist with managing everyday issues and incidents. There are many aspects that can be put to the test including challenging communicators to be able to identify an emerging issue, the ability to be able to step in and put an initial intervention in place, as well as reviewing scenarios to create escalation plans. This does not have to involve huge, complex exercises. It can be as simple as having a scenario to review at each team meeting. The suggested actions can be discussed and approaches reviewed. Chapter 8 will look at the ways we can learn from issues and incidents and improve our approach on an ongoing basis.

CASE STUDY

What happened?

In September 2020, actor John Boyega announced on Twitter that he was stepping down from a role as global brand ambassador for Jo Malone perfume. In a series of tweets, he said: 'Their decision to replace my campaign in China by using my concepts and substituting a local brand ambassador for me, without either my consent or prior notice, was wrong. The film celebrated my personal story – showcasing my hometown, including my friends, and featuring my family. While many brands understandably use a variety of global and local ambassadors, dismissively trading out one's culture this way is not something I can condone.'[7]

What prompted this action was when the company behind the brand, Estée Lauder, removed him from an aftershave advert that was being shown in China. The advert was originally directed, written by and featured Mr Boyega. It was based around his personal story of growing up in southeast London. He was replaced in the advert in China by local brand ambassador for Jo Malone perfume, actor Liu Haoran. The revised advert still retained many of the same concepts shown in the original.

Jo Malone herself came out to criticize the actions of the company at the end of the week that had started with Mr Boyega stepping down. Her intervention came despite the fact that she had sold the brand bearing her name to Estée Lauder in 1999. Estée Lauder later apologized both to Mr Boyega and Mr Haoran. In a statement to the *Hollywood Reporter*, Jo Malone perfume said: 'While we immediately took action and removed the local version of the campaign, we recognize that this was painful, and that offence was caused. We respect John and support our partners and fans globally. We are taking this misstep very seriously and we are working together as a brand to do better moving forward.'[8]

The case highlights the need to have a diverse range of voices involved in communication and to be able to step outside the business to gather opinions and views. Decisions that were made in this case needed to have been reviewed from different perspectives. There were opportunities to prevent this issue emerging including letting others review the proposal before the advert was made and shared. It also is a reminder that self-awareness is critical so there is an understanding of the biases and views that may influence our judgements and decision making. The use of a process of decision making, a flowchart and an escalation plan could assist in preventing the situation developing further by building in reflection time.

KEY LEARNING POINTS

- Ensure diverse voices are involved in developing proactive and reactive communication. Build the systems and networks that allow this to happen swiftly when an issue begins to develop or emerge.
- Take time to reflect on the risks of the communication activity you are involved in. A few moments taking yourself out of the situation to then come back to it may help to highlight areas of concern. Once the risks and concerns are identified, decisions can be taken about how to progress.
- Be aware of the biases and ways that your decision making is influenced. Self-awareness is vital for communicators as it will identify potential problem areas that require further consideration or additional support when responding.
- Systems and processes can support effective decision making by moving people away from relying on instincts, past experiences and a pressure to deliver quickly when developing the next steps. Taking time to use these systems when there is no immediate pressure will assist in training for moving quickly when under pressure.
- An escalation plan will ensure interventions can happen quickly as the situation develops. This would have assisted Estée Lauder, as the problem developed on social media and then led to an increase in news reporting internationally.

Conclusion

Managing emerging issues requires a good understanding of how to make decisions effectively. It is not appropriate to use instincts and 'gut feelings' to develop an action plan to respond to the situation. Communicators need to develop self-awareness and be clear what factors influence their decision making. This will highlight where additional support or assistance is needed to improve what they do. Brands and businesses need to be able to listen to diverse voices from outside the organization. These voices can assist both proactive and reactive communication and should be used when issues are developing. Putting systems in place to consult with those outside the business should be a priority if they do not already exist. Where they do exist, it is important to ensure they can address all the required elements.

Communicators can use systems to look more objectively at the issue that is emerging, questioning their assumptions and highlighting the data, insight and information they need to develop the response. A systematic approach can help people to keep calm when facing the pressure to act decisively, maintain confidence in the business, and minimize reputational damage. Building these systems assists in moving to establish an escalation plan. Recognize when further communication activity may be required following an initial decision on the form of intervention to take. Considering the triggers for further communication activity supports planning for future scenarios and being ready to move quickly.

Making decisions is often required in a pressurized environment. The business may be under sustained criticism or scrutiny and the communicator must advise about the most appropriate way forward. This is a significant responsibility and the impact this can have on an individual must be understood. Making decisions under such pressure is challenging. Improving our resilience and ability to take action is crucial for all decision makers. There are many ways to build this resilience including training, testing and learning, which will be covered in Chapter 8.

Notes

1 Lumen Learning (2012) Understanding Decision Making, Principles of Management, https://courses.lumenlearning.com/atd-tc3-management/chapter/understanding-decision-making/ (archived at https://perma.cc/ZZP2-KBB3)

2 Likierman, A (2020) The 12 elements of independent judgement for a UK Board, CGI, www.cgi.org.uk/assets/files/research/2021/the-12-elements-of-independent-judgement-for-a-uk-board_18082021.pdf (archived at https://perma.cc/N2UQ-NLQU)

3 Likierman, A and Stern, S (2020) How to exercise your judgement during a pandemic, London Business School, www.london.edu/think/how-to-exercise-your-judgement-during-a-pandemic (archived at https://perma.cc/NK3S-L4NS)

4 Wilke, A and Mata, R, (2012) Heuristics and Biases: A short history of cognitive bias, *Encyclopedia of Human Behaviour*, 2nd Edition, www.sciencedirect.com/topics/neuroscience/cognitive-bias (archived at https://perma.cc/UE8W-MYFA)

5 Mackay, J (2017) Weekly Roundup: 7 cognitive biases that ruin your decision-making process [Blog] *Rescue Time*, 2 November, https://blog.rescuetime.com/7-cognitive-biases-decision-making/ (archived at https://perma.cc/YGE8-ZD99)

6 Drucker, P (1967) The Effective Decision, *Harvard Business Review*, January, www.hbr.org/1967/01/the-effective-decision (archived at https://perma.cc/NF77-U8JK)

7 Boyega, J (2020) Their decision to replace my campaign in China by using my concepts and substituting a local brand ambassador for me, without either my consent or prior notice, was wrong, September 2020. No longer available as account has been closed.

8 Kilkenny, K (2020) John Boyega stepping down as Jo Malone brand ambassador, *The Hollywood Reporter*, 14 September, www.hollywoodreporter.com/news/general-news/john-boyega-stepping-down-as-jo-malone-brand-ambassador-4060225/ (archived at https://perma.cc/9AZW-A72M)

8

Learning from issues and incidents

Introduction

Being able to effectively deal with the day-to-day problems and issues that emerge is built upon effectively learning from what has happened before. It is a wasted opportunity to fail to build in review and evaluation of the situation that has been faced. Once the problem has been eradicated or contained it is important to capture the learning and details of the experience. This chapter will consider what information to gather and review, how to develop systems to bring learning back into the workplace, and how to move forward making necessary changes. Consistently reviewing what happened and detailing what can be learnt can help prevent re-running the same problems repeatedly.

Steps can be taken to make changes, improve elements, and build understanding about ongoing problems that will aid business developments. Taking the time to reflect on the problem, management of it and communication associated with it will improve your future responses to situations. Aspects that worked can be highlighted and where problems occurred, they can be assessed to support future decision making. All this improves the future reaction to developing issues. If there is an opportunity to prevent a recurrence of the situation this can also be highlighted. The more problems that can be neutralized or eradicated, the easier it will be to devote time to identifying those new situations that develop.

The information that is gathered should be put into the business to support its development. Where a product or service needs to be revised, or where new systems and processes need to be created, this should be documented and dealt with. Organizations need to develop ways to capture the learning from situations and build them into processes, policies and procedures. The information should also be introduced to the risk management processes as it provides an early warning of possible challenges that may lie ahead if there are no changes.

Reviewing situations once they are concluded is not just a stage for crisis management and should be undertaken with everyday problems and issues. Everything that was introduced to manage the issue, the impact it did or did not have, and the way communication operated should be put under the microscope. Review needs to consider the way the situation escalated and what procedures were used, what communication took place with the media, social media, internally with staff, and with stakeholders and others. A critical element is to consider the relationships that were used to support the response but also to identify where they could be improved so that effective connections are in place across the business.

Finally, the time to reflect will help to improve the way communication is developed and delivered. It can support the training of staff and creation of a more effective response to future situations that may emerge. This is a crucial step that can break the cycle of problem, action, resolution which then goes back to a re-emergence of the problem. Without this step organizations will keep doing the same things and get the same results. This will prevent the chance of moving forward so it is important to embrace the learning and the opportunity to do things differently.

Measuring the impact

Learning from events can only happen if you have a clear understanding of whether the interventions worked. Evaluating the activity undertaken is critical. It is a fundamental element of PR, and this does not change when you are managing issues or even tackling a crisis. The same steps of identifying the communication objectives at the start of the issues management and then considering the outputs, outtakes and outcomes can be utilized. The AMEC Framework provides a structure that can support the evaluation of issues.[1] If there are already systems to evaluate communication within the business then review how they can be used when assessing the success of issues management. Ensure that evaluation is undertaken as the first step towards reviewing and learning from the experience.

The evaluation measures used will depend on the objectives that were detailed at the start of the communication activity. Remember to assess if these changed when further interventions were required. The following six points can assist in considering the impact of the activity when conducting the evaluation:

1 **Reaching a satisfactory conclusion**
   As the issue emerges and you are developing the approach to take including any escalation plan, clearly outline the outcome towards which you are working. This will be the finish line that you are hoping to reach through the communication activity. It is important to be realistic but also stretching. Avoid a negative approach focusing just on damage limitation as there may be opportunities within the situation.

2 **Minimizing the impact on people**
   A critical factor in all communication and especially as an issue has emerged is to understand the impact it has on people. Who is affected by what has happened? How many people are affected? Where are they based? What have they got to say about the situation? The evaluation should review how people were affected by the situation. Essentially, has the communication intervention and activity had a positive impact and minimized the impact on people? This is not just an issue for the operational response to consider. Look to identify what the communication has done to address criticism, build confidence and restore trust in the brand.

3 Minimizing the impact on the brand/business

Assess the way communication has supported the business and helped to maintain or improve its position. This could be through market share, product confidence, or share price being stable or increasing. Some brands are strong enough to weather serious incidents and issues, for example large multinationals like Amazon and Apple. In that case the damage from situations will be minimal but it remains important to review the response to ensure any early alert to developments and changes that may be required is gathered.

4 Positive engagement through social media

There are, as seen in Chapter 6, many ways in which social media is an important medium for communication when dealing with a problem. Analytics from the channels can give a wide range of data including reach, impact and engagement. It is the engagement that is a critical measurement, as is having a positive conversation and interaction. Remember to consider both the qualitative and quantitative information when reviewing the use of social media.

5 Reflection of the narrative/key messages in the media

Evaluating the success of engagements with the media can be more problematic than assessing social media interactions. In many cases lack of coverage within the media is part of the satisfactory conclusion of the issue. If there is coverage, the prominence and use of the narrative or key messages that have been developed is important when evaluating. It is also valuable to review the feedback to the coverage, comments on news media websites, and how it has impacted on people's views of the situation and of the business.

6 Supportive feedback from key groups, e.g. stakeholders, shareholders, politicians, public

If there has been feedback from influential groups this can be valuable to the evaluation. The groups may be stakeholders, shareholders, political leaders, sections of the public or employees, and their support for the response and action that has been taken should be gathered. The views will assist in gathering feedback away from the confines of social media or the news media. Be clear which groups are the most influential for the business and the issue that has occurred. For example, if you have a problem at a premises run by the business, then a key group will be the residents and those in the immediate vicinity of the premises. Understand where key groups and individuals are for both the business and for the issue being managed.

Managing an issue is not just about minimizing damage and any impact on confidence in the brand or business. Every issue can provide opportunities for the organization. There may be the chance to increase market share, to improve reputation, to promote the brand to a new audience, and many other elements. This will not be done by failing to listen to the voices that are concerned about the issue, or not facing up to the situation. But an effective response can provide a chance to do things differently, to improve the business, and to build for a stronger future. This can be difficult to quantify but will be part of the review and learning from the issue and its management. If the situation is satisfactorily concluded at an early stage with no public recognition of it, then documenting it is still important. It is a 'near miss', which is a moment when an issue or problem is averted and the damaging position that could have happened is halted. Gathering information about these moments is also critical. 'Near misses' will be discussed later in this chapter.

Starting to review

When beginning to assess the impact and aftermath of an issue it is helpful to take a systematic approach to ensure no elements are forgotten. Start by looking at what happened, what decisions were made and what processes were used. Look for patterns in both the situation and the communication. Identifying patterns helps us to see where problems occurred or where interventions could have been made. Understand what led the issue to emerge and what caused it to develop. This is essential information for the business as it can point the way to change to safeguard against it happening again. For the communicator it is essential to assess how and when the identification of the issue happened. Could it have been spotted earlier? Did it highlight a failure with the existing monitoring systems? What improvements could be made to speed up the identification process? This, as has been highlighted in Chapter 1, is the foundation to support an effective response to those everyday situations.

Consider who was involved and affected by the situation. Understand if they caused the emergence of the issue in some way. Did they bring it to the attention of the business? Was it a complaint that they made about a problem they were experiencing? Identifying those involved also necessitates an understanding of the scale of the impact on them. At this point do not forget to chart those who were involved from the business and were involved in the response. Ask who should have been involved if this was different to those who did respond, and also look at how things could have been improved if others had been called to assist. Review the time things happened to understand if there was something significant about it. Could the issue be linked to a certain time of year, time of day or date in the calendar? As well as helping to identify things to consider in the future to prevent a further occurrence, signposting to trigger points can also help in improving the response. How long the problem ran before it was concluded is also significant. This leads to the most important aspect to review, which is the actions that were taken, the decisions that were made, and what could have been done differently.

Areas to review

Chart the steps that were taken from the first moment the issue became evident. If there was a lack of action, consider whether that was the most appropriate step to take. Assess whether it may have been possible to reduce the impact the issue had or to eradicate it completely if a different course of action had been taken. This can be done using data and insight provided from those connected to the response. It is beneficial to ask others for their view of the situation and how it was handled to obtain an objective perspective. The three key questions in any review are: 1) What worked in the response? 2) What did not work during the response? 3) What could have been done differently? If the review has to be undertaken at speed, then use the three questions to keep focused on what to quickly assess before moving forward. Gathering views will assist with all three questions, as will reviewing the decisions that were made and how they were made. Reflect on the decision-making process outlined in Chapter 7 to unpick what happened and the rationale behind decisions that were made.

In looking at the situation, take time to consider how you can prevent it from emerging again and to understand if there are any legacy issues linked to what happened. There may be aspects of the problem that require further action at some future date. Ensure that this is noted so that it can be addressed at that point to prevent further issues or the problem re-emerging. For example, if there was a problem with a product and it has been rectified but there is a report on the situation that is going to be published, be aware of the dates. Understand what may be published and be ready to communicate about it, particularly if the issue was public. The business will face potential criticism for failing to disclose the details of such reports and those who were affected may become vocal again on social media or within the news media about a perceived 'cover up', leading to another issue to manage. Communication can support the business to identify changes needed to prevent a recurrence of the problem. Use the review to consider changes to make, policies to amend, training that may be required, and processes that may need to be introduced. Perhaps additional manufacturing checks would prevent faulty items coming to market, or a policy on the use of social media alongside appropriate training would minimize the risks of staff making inappropriate postings. An effective review will look at all such elements to help improve the business.

Finally, consider within the communication the two key aspects of channels and messages. What impact did the messages have on the situation, and did they work? Assess whether some of the wording may have inflamed the situation; perhaps the mood and tone of the communication made the problem worse. Did the channels reach the right people or were there problems in making connections to key audiences? If the business has challenges in reaching certain communities with proactive communication, this situation will still be the same when an issue is being managed. Use the review of the response to identify positive changes that can be made to help day-to-day communication activity and to be more prepared to respond when issues emerge.

Daily learning systems

The review and learning do not have to become a burden that takes a significant amount of time to complete. While it is important that this phase takes place it does not need to be a lengthy and complex process that puts additional pressure on an already busy team. If you have many critical or challenging issues to deal with in a week then it can become too problematic to review each of them and try to conduct detailed debriefs. Debriefs are a critical part of the crisis communication review process and need to be undertaken when moving forward from serious situations and emergencies. For everyday issues it is important to take the principles of these debriefs and put a system in place that can be used quickly and at any point during the working week. It is vital that this is approached as a learning opportunity and not as a chance to look for where to apportion blame. Being open to developing is a mindset that needs to be developed as well as using issues to refine communication and approaches that are taken. There are a number of ways that this mindset can be introduced in day-to-day work.

Review daily decisions

Note your decision making on communication issues every day. Use a database or computer system that will allow the input of information about what was happening and why a particular decision was taken. This can assist when decisions are made before the issue develops. Consider how you approached the decision making, particularly in the initial stages or when facing a complex situation. Look at the impact of the decisions to consider where improvements could be made.

Create a meeting structure

Develop a system where the decisions and actions can be reviewed. This may be part of existing risk management meetings or organizational development activity. The aim is to look at incidents, issues and trends, considering where links may exist. It is this meeting that can consider business developments and changes that may be required following post-incident reviews. This should take place on a six-monthly or quarterly basis and is not about dealing with immediate actions but instead looking at the longer-term requirements. This meeting can help people to see the bigger picture as different departments may have pieces of a jigsaw that will build to show the problem that needs to be addressed.

Discuss with other teams

Internal communication has a key role to play when considering how to learn and develop the way issues are managed. Understand what issues teams are concerned about and are focused on preparing to manage. But it is also a way to look at how they are responding and managing situations, and what communication could do to assist. Sharing information, trends and learning from situations can help everyone to be more prepared to effectively manage those emerging issues. Having a two-way conversation with departments across the organization and really listening to their position, strengthens the issues management process.

Consider plans

Development sessions and planning days can support the learning about managing everyday situations. They can skill the team by allowing discussion about scenarios and how they may be approached.

Considering scenarios is not just something for crisis preparedness; it can be used in many other circumstances. There is an opportunity to test existing plans and assess where there are areas for development. It can also be used to gauge how aware the communication team are of plans and approaches to issues management. Start by considering the last four issues you had to manage and look at what you did and what you could do differently. Alternatively, look at five regular problems that businesses face: complaints about services or products, staff being trolled on social media, concern about a campaign developed, a senior manager making inappropriate comments to the media or online, and anger about a business policy such as on the environment, and consider how you would approach them.

Assess the industry landscape

Every business looks at what is happening within their industry to consider the latest trends and developments. This same environmental scanning is an important way to learn about how to approach and respond to situations. Look at what is happening in competitors' businesses and in the wider sector. Where there are challenges, complaints or problems, review the response that is taken and see what you can learn for your own situations. Considering the approaches others take and assessing the response is an important part of the learning process. Understand the data and insight.

Reputation management has to start with a clear understanding of what your reputation looks like and what people feel and think about the business. Understand your reputation and chart it for all communication activity. If you do not know whether people have trust and confidence in the brand or organization, how can you confidently develop communication strategies and plans for proactive and reactive work? Understanding your position and where it is in the wider environment will help in tracking the impact of activity to respond to issues. Know where the data exists on this, how you can access it, and how to revise it when needed.

Train the organization about issues communication

Communicators often carry out work behind closed doors and only occasionally will explain the work they do. Busy teams put talking about communication and what it brings to the business to the bottom of any 'to do' list. Everyone from the CEO through to the frontline staff should know what to do when issues emerge, what their role is, and how communication teams are going to respond. Training employees and empowering them to act quickly to limit the impact of a problem is essential. Review the operations in the business and how they work. Consider who would benefit from training to enable them to step up and act.

Explore consultation

The importance of diverse voices and listening to others has been mentioned throughout this book; it is a crucial element to learning. Talking to those from outside the business, whether customers, stakeholders or others, can help with understanding the reputational standing of the business. It can highlight any changes due to issues and incidents. People can help to quality-assure approaches that are being considered, highlight any gaps, and provide valuable insight. Remember to maximize the consultation opportunities that exist within the business and use them for the benefit of communication.

Failing to learn from experiences can lead to similar problems occurring in the future. Without structure around the debrief, review and learning, the business risks blundering into the same situations over and over again. This can be seen in the Canadian Revenue Agency case study in Chapter 2.[2] If a problem is seen once then action should be taken to ensure that the same situation does not happen again. For example, if the business is told that a customer service system is failing and people are unable to get issues rectified, then something should be done to improve the service or prepare for a worsening position and a growing number of complaints. Such situations can impact on sales and damage the reputation of the business.

TOP TIP

Keep a database of risks and issues that have been dealt with in the past and may appear in the future. It needs to be designed to work for you and the business. You may use a simple spreadsheet or database. How it looks is not critical but ensuring it covers the information you need is essential. If there are many risks and issues to be considered keep a separate spreadsheet for each area of risk with key points from previous problems and the management of them. Use the information gathered from other departments, risk management information, and information that is identified on a daily basis and keep the spreadsheet as a living document. Everyone in the communication team should have access to it so they can be aware of the issues within it. Proactive communication can work to prevent problems occurring in the first place if you are aware of situations you are working to avoid. Cross-check the information that is included in this repository with data from social media, customer services or other insight from the business.

Issues become the change

With any issue or problem that is managed comes the opportunity to make changes to the business and to communication. The principles of effective change management also support effective issues management. There are five steps to change management:

1   **Understand and acknowledge that there is a need to change**
    This can be done through the review and evaluation phase of the response. Use the quarterly meeting and updates to the business to demonstrate what is required and explain why. Data and information from specific issues and problems should be used to gain support from senior leaders for the need to change.

2   **Communicate the need to change and involve people in the development**
    Recognize the involvement of others and capture a diverse range of views to improve the change management process. Be clear

what happened, what needs to change, and importantly, why it needs to change. This should be a compelling explanation of why the change is needed.

3 Develop the plans for change
Use the information and views to document what the change is and how it will support the business. Be clear about the steps needed to make the change and who will be involved. Be practical in outlining how to make the transition and embed the change.

4 Implement the plans for change
Make the plan a reality and continue to make the connection with why the change is needed. Refer back to the compelling argument for why the change is needed but also to the benefits for employees and the business. Focus on connecting to the human benefits from the change that is being implemented.

5 Evaluate the progress and promote any success from the change
Monitor the impact of the change and what benefits it has brought to employees and the business. If the change has led to the prevention of problems or issues emerging, share it with the business. Be clear how things have been improved with tangible examples wherever possible.

The approach to change management goes hand in hand with dealing with everyday issues and problems. The situation does not have to be a serious and critical problem to require change to happen within the business in its aftermath. Review your current issues management and consider how change could be introduced and at what stage. Are there systems in place that allow changes to be proposed by the communication team? Consider what more the communication function could do to become more effective in managing day-to-day incidents. When everyday issues are addressed, responded to, reviewed and learnt from, a business becomes stronger. It builds its market position and reputation.

Near misses matter

There are many occasions when an issue or problem is spotted but does not develop further; an area of concern is identified but then disappears without any action being taken, or an initial intervention brings it to a conclusion without any further steps. These are 'near misses' – where a problem emerges but does not fully develop. Look at how to learn from these situations. They are unlikely to appear on the issue and risk spreadsheet you may have, or be part of any review or debrief. But they provide an early warning to a situation that may develop, a future problem, or a view that is evolving. So, how can you capture the information from these near misses?

Start by creating a culture where people recognize near misses and make a note of them as part of awareness raising and monitoring of trends. Consider it like the accident reporting in many big organizations, where not only accidents are reported but also the near misses – moments when an accident was averted. This information helps to give communicators a focus for where issues may be developing and could emerge in the future. Plans and strategies can be developed, and pre-emptive action may be carried out. For example, if there is a distribution problem emerging which has led to some emails from customers, and this is managed in the short term, it is a warning that further work may be required in this area. If the distribution problem cannot be managed to prevent it happening again then effective communication activity may help to mitigate the impact of it on customers.

Assessing if there was an issue

Five elements that are in place when there is an issue that is developing and becoming a problem should be kept at the forefront of your thoughts:

1 Something has failed whether it is a product or service or a response from the business.
2 The situation is detrimentally affecting people.

3 The issue will be of interest to the public.

4 The business has been slow to respond, failed to respond, or is perceived to have failed to address the issue as it developed.

5 There is a lack of responsibility for what is emerging.

If these elements are becoming evident, there is still an opportunity to intervene and act. Direct communication or the reshaping of communication can still stop the situation worsening. Look at what it means both now and in the immediate future. Refocusing the proactive communication and the business's communication strategy should be considered quarterly or at least every six months. Ask if there are issues and near misses that have been identified that require a change in the approach to the communication or some campaigns and initiatives. Look at what further action could be taken to strengthen the response to everyday problems and to build and protect the organization's reputation. This work supports moves to be alert to what the future may bring.

Failing to act on these 'near misses' will put the business at risk of moving to a full-blown incident or crisis. At this point the damage is likely to be more severe to the operation of the business, the share price, and its reputation. It makes focusing on data and understanding the threats and risks that may lie ahead critical for communicators. Being able to recognize the trends that may be of concern and have an escalation process ready to support action is essential.

Issues management every day

PR and communication have always been focused on promoting the business, supporting developments, enhancing reputation and creating innovative campaigns and promotions. The daily approach is to seek out opportunities for communication and to positively build the reputation of the business. In March 2020, the Covid-19 pandemic changed the way that communicators viewed the work they do. Managing issues and incidents suddenly became a daily requirement and understanding crisis communication a critical skill for all communicators. This was highlighted in the UK Government Communication Service-led report from the Covid-19 Communications Advisory Panel Report.[3] Communicators need to keep challenges and issues at the front of their mind whilst at the same time continuing with core promotional activity. As mentioned earlier this can be done through weekly briefings and discussions about emerging trends and issues, but the education and training programme should start when someone joins the organization. Provide new starters with an outline of the approach taken to issues management and crisis communication. Bring the conversation about issues and their management into the day-to-day work. This does not need to take a huge amount of time but is about remaining alert to ensure reviews and monitoring continue.

Make issues management part of the training plan for the communication team, or for yourself. Put it within the communication objective-setting each year, and ensure it is part of discussions about communication strategies. To engage the team in this approach to communication, keep making opportunities out of potential issues and problems at the heart of discussions. It can feel that the focus on issues and problems stifles creativity so turn it around and show how tackling issues brings opportunities to grow creatively. Induction is the right time to explain systems and processes that exist within the communication function. It is an opportunity to discuss how issues management operates and the role that the new member of staff can play. Explain about the monitoring of issues, the principles of the response, and how escalation works within communication. Providing recruits with this detail, as well as additional training opportunities, puts them in the right place to understand what to do from day one.

For those involved in developing specialist campaigns and initiatives, encourage them to build issues management into their workplans, campaigns and strategies. This means considering and documenting the risks and issues that may occur when the work is implemented. Identify how things will be managed, mitigated or raised higher if more drastic action is needed, and consider who will take responsibility for managing any problems. For example, if a campaign is developed to promote a changed recipe for a much-loved product, the strategy should consider what to do if people respond negatively to the change and also if they dislike the campaign in some way. Look at what could be amended or adapted within the campaign to take account of negative feedback, and the additional work that may be required to turn the situation around. The nature of the response will vary depending on the organization's appetite for risk. Some businesses are ready to accept more risks than others and are prepared to ride out issues that emerge.

The role of leaders

Leaders within a business have a vital role to play in effective issues management. They must demonstrate the principles of openness and being accountable when managing problems. This is vital for developing a 'no blame' culture and one that listens and is ready to accept responsibility when something goes wrong. Those at the top of the business also need to demonstrate a commitment to understanding the latest trends and issues that may affect the smooth running of the business. They need to be aware of the environmental scanning in the same way they are the financial information. Communicators have a key role in ensuring this happens. They should focus on developing relationships that give them the ear of the board and CEO and sharing essential information about issues and problems they have handled. The effective CEO and top team want to understand what people think, what the reputation of the business is and to see how things can be improved. This will assist them when considering future changes and developments within the business. Creating a culture of problem solving and issues management within the business should be supported by those at the top demonstrating the approach they want to see from all staff. It is important to walk the walk, not to just say what is required but to really show it in how they listen to concerns. Involvement from the top team at the quarterly risk and issues management meetings is an important way to demonstrate this commitment. Any CEO that is unwilling to get involved with or is disinterested in issues management should be reminded that failing to manage problems can lead to serious consequences and could lead the business into crisis.

The communicator's personal development

Training for the communication team is important but so is building a personal development plan that will help the communicator in the post-pandemic world. They are facing an increasingly uncertain world where people are more aware of issues, incidents and crises. This uncertainty is challenging for the business environment, putting additional pressure on all employees. For communicators, they need to be monitoring for issues, ready to respond and able to make critical decisions quickly. This means reviewing current development plans to ensure they are supporting individuals to manage issues more effectively. There are six key areas of personal development that should be considered:

1 **Risk management**
   Communicators need to understand how to manage risks and develop communication that can support this. They need to be able to identify risks and issues and see how risks present challenges and opportunities. Set the management of risks by the communication team within the wider risk management work undertaken by the organization.

2 **Understanding communities**
   Bringing diverse voices into the development of communication and the response to issues is a key skill. It requires an understanding of consultation and community engagement, and how it can improve communication. As well as understanding audiences and customers, the communicators should see expansively and understand communities affected.

3 **Business knowledge**
   Effective issues identification and management requires a good understanding of how the business operates. Communicators

need this in-depth detail to be able to elevate the communication activity beyond product promotion campaigns. They need to be able to talk the language of the business, from IT and finance to HR and product development.

4 Governance and planning

The way the business is managed and how it runs planning cycles are also key areas to understand as part of personal development. It is only by truly understanding how power operates throughout the business that communication can start to become involved. Communication planning, communication strategy development and review should all sit within business governance.

5 Influencing

Communicators need to be heard when there is challenging information to share. They need to be heard by those at the top of the business and be in the position where they can share information about issues and encourage others to act. It is not just about promoting communication but also demonstrating expertise, gaining authority, and operating strategically.

6 Decision making

As covered in Chapter 7, effective decision making is a key area of development for communicators who will be involved in issues management. They need to have a process to operate within and to be aware of what may impact on their own judgement. This development can assist with all work and not just issues management.

Communicators should critically assess their abilities in each of these areas, then identify where there are areas for development. Those aspects should then feature in the personal development plan. Underpinning these requirements is the need to build personal resilience so that the response can be developed quickly, the negativity does not impact on those responding, and they can maintain perspective on situations.

CASE STUDY

What happened?

In June 2021, a group of ex-employees from the brewery company BrewDog posted an open letter on Twitter using the account @punkswithpurpose.[4] The account had more than 13,000 followers and began posting in June 2021, even though it had been set up on the social media site a year earlier. The letter accused the beer company of operating a 'culture of fear', bullying staff and treating employees 'like objects'.[5] The letter continued by claiming there was a toxic culture at the business and that it had impacted on the mental wellbeing of staff. There were further allegations made involving health and safety and that the company values were not reflected in the workplace. Much of the criticism was directed at BrewDog co-founder James Watt, who the group claimed was personally responsible for the 'rotten culture'.[6]

Even the development of the response was put under the microscope. The *Guardian* newspaper reported that they had seen an internal staff memo that indicated there was consideration given to encouraging current employees to sign a response letter, but this tactic had not been progressed.[7] Instead of this approach, BrewDog released a statement acknowledging some of the failings that had been highlighted.[8] The statement said the company were committed to doing better and apologized, but added that thousands of employees had positive stories. It continued to say that action would be taken. A week after this happened James Watt spoke on his LinkedIn page and promised an independent review of the situation.[9] He said action would also include an anonymous staff survey, exit interviews and a salary review, and he made a further apology to staff.

In an interview with the BBC, Watt spoke very quickly but his tone appeared dismissive of the situation and it felt as though he was trying to move forward too swiftly.[10] The coverage also led to concerns being raised by some of the many investors in the company who had invested more than £80 million. The company had 180,000 crowdfunding investors that had helped its growth to become the UK's largest craft brewer.[11]

KEY LEARNING POINTS

- Know your risks and the issues that may affect the business so that you can consider response strategies. This should also include creating escalation plans that allow for the development of communication to address the way the issue is evolving. In the case of BrewDog, the possibility of staff criticizing the company could have been foreseen and steps taken to prepare a response plan.

- Monitor the issues that you deal with and be alert to them re-emerging at some point in the future. Each business will have a certain set of ongoing challenges that may be due to products, services, staff, leadership, governance, or other aspects of the operation. Being aware of them will help communicators to be alert to signs of developing problems. The creation of the Twitter page for @punkswithpurpose a year earlier may have been an alert to a growing problem.

- Learn from each issue that is managed so that the response is improved in future recurrences. At every opportunity after an issue, consider what worked well, what could be improved, and where things should be done differently. In January 2022, the BBC ran a documentary looking at the allegations about BrewDog. It led to James Watt talking about taking legal action against the documentary makers and criticizing ex-employees who spoke on the programme.[12] This appears to be a similar approach to ones made when the situation emerged rather than developing the response further.

- Respond quickly when there are signs of a problem developing so that you can avoid it becoming a full-blown crisis. Taking some small steps to show an acceptance that there is an issue, and providing some immediate actions that can mitigate the impact on people, can allow time to develop a more detailed and comprehensive communication and response plan. In the coverage of the BrewDog situation there appear to have been mixed messages despite apologies being given.

- Avoid blaming others when the organization should be open, honest, and accountable for its part in the issue developing. Being positive within the communication can limit the impact of the situation. But setting up a position that disagrees with the situation and what it highlights is likely to extend the problem and lead to an escalation of the issue. In the statements and responses made by BrewDog there was a conflict between the recognition of the problems and an apology, and criticism of those who highlighted concerns.

Conclusion

When issues occur, it is not enough to just deal with them and avoid them growing into a critical incident or crisis. We must learn from them and gather data and insight that can be shared with the business to support future developments. Reviewing what happened to lead to the issue emerging and the impact of the response provides valuable insight. This is information that should be provided to the decision makers within the organization. Environmental scanning is enhanced when it takes account of the problems that teams have been handling. Even if they are seen as 'low level' problems they can be a sign of bigger issues to come. Communicators need to create a simple system that will allow them to undertake swift reviews and to identify both how to improve the response and what the issue may signify for the business.

Building issues management into the day-to-day work of communication teams is an effective way of ensuring problems are recognized, identified and managed. Ensure those joining the team are given the relevant information and support to keep them alert to situations that may develop. Discuss issues management in communication planning and strategy days, and when monitoring activities within the team. The understanding of issues management can be improved when it is talked about within everyday business. Where necessary introduce training days and encourage the team to create their own development plans that will support them in learning more about this area. Spend time reviewing scenarios and considering the actions that could be taken. Look at the way communication may need to develop to try and manage the impact of the situation. And during training consider what the impact of failing to manage issues may be on the business operation, financial stability, and reputation.

Do not ignore near misses and problems that fail to develop; they are a valuable source of insight and information. They may be a signpost to a problem that could re-emerge in the future and could require careful management. Develop systems that allow the team, and others in the business, to document near misses and issues that they manage. Use the governance processes within the business to raise these issues up so that they can inform the development of the organization. Find the space to allow the team to reflect on the situations that they are faced with so that they do not rush ahead making quick decisions on what to do. Being able to take a moment to look at the options available and consider an escalation plan can provide a more effective response to everyday issues.

Notes

1 AMEC Online, Integrated Evaluation Framework, www.amecorg.com/amecframework/framework/interactive-framework/ (archived at https://perma.cc/FRC9-55ZK)

2 Government of Canada (nd), Cyber Incidents, www.canada.ca/en/revenue-agency/news/2020/09/cyber-incidents.html (archived at https://perma.cc/KD8M-RCSD)

3 UK Government (2020) Introducing the Covid-19 Communication Advisory Panel report, https://gcs.civilservice.gov.uk/news/introducing-the-covid-19-communications-advisory-panel-report/ (archived at https://perma.cc/ZU7V-6AJL)

4 Punks with Purpose (2021) An open letter to BrewDog [Twitter] 9 June, https://twitter.com/PunksWPurpose/status/1402724680637747200 (archived at https://perma.cc/YM3F-VEUF)

5 BBC News Online (2021) Ex-Brewdog staff allege culture of fear at brewer, 10 June, www.bbc.co.uk/news/business-57428258 (archived at https://perma.cc/AA6X-RQ4H)

6 Drinks Retailing (2021) BrewDog 'sorry' for 'rotten culture', 11 June, https://drinksretailingnews.co.uk/news/fullstory.php/aid/20489/BrewDog_sorry_for_rotten_culture_.html (archived at https://perma.cc/88NY-57G2)

7 Makortoff, K and Davies, R (2021) Former BrewDog staff accuse craft beer firm of culture of fear, *Guardian*, 10 June, https://www.theguardian.com/business/2021/jun/10/brewdog-staff-craft-beer-firm-letter (archived at https://perma.cc/3V9X-ANQG)

8 Webster, L (2021) Brewdog CEO responds to open letter from ex-employees criticising company, *The National*, 10 June, https://www.thenational.scot/news/19362954.brewdog-ceo-responds-open-letter-ex-employees-criticising-company/ (archived at https://perma.cc/GMV6-PX8A)

9 Watt, J (2021) The Road Ahead for BrewDog [LinkedIn] 17 June, https://www.linkedin.com/pulse/road-ahead-brewdog-james-watt (archived at https://perma.cc/G3SF-G9NP)

10 BBC News Online (2021) Brewdog boss vows to learn after 'toxic culture' criticism, 11 June, https://www.bbc.co.uk/news/business-57434978 (archived at https://perma.cc/E66A-NNCL)

11 Evans, J, Hancock, A and O'Dwyer, M (2021) Punk rebellion: BrewDog's crowdfunding investors start to lose faith, *Financial Times*, 25 June, https://www.ft.com/content/5ad0e222-a35b-4ae8-aa16-27f1feb964a5 (archived at https://perma.cc/KPB7-6E4M)

12 Patterson, S (2022) Brewer's Strop: BrewDog founder James Watt threatens to sue BBC over upcoming Disclosure doc probing craft beer giant's 'toxic culture', *Scottish Sun*, 21 January, https://www.thescottishsun.co.uk/news/scottish-news/8315674/brewdog-james-watt-bbc-disclosure-documentary/ (archived at https://perma.cc/78J6-5LCD)

9

Incident scenarios to consider

Introduction

Having looked at the aspects of managing an issue we will now consider how to put these elements into practice. In Chapter 8, the role of scenario planning and developing staff was highlighted and this can start using the details in the scenarios that follow. This chapter will detail five of the most frequent issues that can affect both businesses and communication teams. The fictionalized situations will develop and require action to be taken once the initial response has been made. After outlining the situation that has developed, details of steps for communicators to take will be provided. These scenarios can be used to help train and develop staff, encouraging them to consider their own decision making and the actions that could be taken. Examples like the ones included are a useful way of testing understanding of the approach to issues management among staff, but also to develop an awareness of what to consider.

Each of the five scenarios is a situation that could appear at any point and require action to be taken. The way these situations are identified, addressed and managed will define whether they are seen as effective issues management. The scenarios have a number of inputs which are created to replicate the way in which situations develop in reality. Minimizing the impact of the issue on the business, its operation and reputation should be at the heart of the responses. Remember that situations can develop because of a lack of action, and reflect on the principles of intervention outlined in Chapter 4. In working through the scenarios try to put yourself into the position of being called to provide advice and support to an organization you are working with or for.

Scenario one

Input 1

A post appears on social media that claims the business's website is down and that customers are unable to place orders. More than that, people who have problems with existing orders cannot make changes or get a response. This is highlighted in two more social media posts. Each of the posts is from a different account run by a different person. Each of the posts is identified through the general social media monitoring that is carried out by the business. The website is run by a different department and there has been no indication that there are any problems with the way it is operating. This is a busy morning and you are organizing the launch of a new product due to take place tomorrow, which means the team are focused on ensuring that everything is ready and in place. They are speaking to the media about the launch and preparing the key spokesperson from the product development team.

WHAT WOULD YOU DO?

In the first instance understand whether there is a genuine problem developing. Contacting the website team is an urgent first step to understanding whether they are dealing with an issue and may have failed to make others in the business aware. Remember not to panic. The team need to continue to prepare for tomorrow's big launch as nothing has yet been confirmed that would necessitate cancelling it. Focus on gathering the facts as quickly as possible. It is advisable to make the communication manager or lead aware that you are handling the situation so that they can be prepared if it develops further. Ensure you have looked at the detail of the posts – what do they say and what can you gather about the situation from the people who have posted? Check whether these accounts have posted about problems before, and if the business has responded to them in the past. Check as well for any additional posts that mention any problems with the website. If there are no problems with the operation of the website, then carefully word a response to those who have raised concerns. It needs to be in the tone and style the business uses on social media but also be clear not to belittle, undermine or attack those raising the issues. At this point, until any problem has been confirmed, the processes for issues management will not be in operation. Management will not have been informed. However, this may be required if, for example, the CEO is an active user of social media and may have been tagged into the complaints. In this situation ensure that the CEO has the latest information about the situation and what you are doing about it.

Consider at this point if you would have done anything different. Would you have dismissed the problems? At what point would you alert the CEO and senior management? And would you have made the team working on the product launch aware of the situation?

Input 2

You speak to the website team, and they say they have just identified a problem with the systems. It is not clear yet what has caused the problem and whether it is a random issue or related to some form of cyber-attack. They are running various checks and should know within the next couple of hours what is behind the problem. At that point they will be able to give details about what action they are going to take and when the website will be back and fully functioning. They ask you whether there is a message you would like to put on the website so that people are aware there is an ongoing problem.

WHAT WOULD YOU DO?

The team have provided clarification that a problem has definitely emerged. But the information is incomplete, and it is not clear how long this may take to rectify. If the situation continues without any communication, you can expect further complaints to be raised.

However, if you communicate you will be highlighting that there is a problem, and a serious cyber-attack and sharing this on social media will also make the news media aware of the problem. Deciding on the action to take needs to start by considering all the information you have and any details that the website team can provide. If there has been a comparable situation in the past look at how it may help in defining the action in this case. Check whether competitors may have faced the same situation in the past. What did they do and how was it received?

Once you have gathered the information it is time to develop a plan and start to consider the scenarios that may develop. Short-term action needs to involve a message asking for customers to be patient while a technical issue is dealt with. If possible, give people an alternative if they have an urgent issue. This may be using a phone line or sharing an email address, if one can be established, that will allow immediate action to be taken where it is needed. The communication team need to be aware that there is a problem and to consider how it may affect the product launch tomorrow, and the key people within the business need to be contacted. Share with them the action that you are taking and explain that scenarios for the future are being considered. There are three main scenarios to review: the situation disappears and access is resumed; the team identify the issue, which is not malicious and can be rectified; and a malicious cyber-attack has affected the website.

Remember to keep social media under review and monitor any queries coming into the communication team from journalists. Keep a check on the news media as the team are talking to them about the launch and they may inadvertently mention the situation. Are they aware of a problem and can they help to share the details of the action that is being taken to continue to provide access to services? At this point it is also important to consider what internal communication may be required, particularly to front-line staff and customer services teams. It is not the right time to start bringing stakeholders into the communication activity, but it is time to start developing a list of people who may need to be contacted if it turns into the most serious situation. Make sure that relevant information is being collated, whether that is from employees, the media, social media or customer services. Start to understand how the situation is being viewed by those outside the business and most importantly those who are most affected. Consider if there are any additional actions that you would have put in place. What would you have included in this early communication plan? Are you able to go proactive to discuss the situation and the response? How will you know if the news media are interested?

Input 3

Around three hours have elapsed, and the website team have been working non-stop to try to fix the problem. The message about the website being down has been shared on social media and is being reported on local news sites and local radio broadcasts. There is speculation growing about whether it is linked to some form of cyber-attack, but the majority of coverage is just alerting people to the situation and the alternative ways to contact the business. The website team contact you to say the site will be back up in 10 minutes and it was a system upgrade that was done overnight and led to some functionality being lost. There is no sign of a data breach or a cyber-attack.

WHAT WOULD YOU DO?

The first thing is to prepare the communication that will be used but delay sending anything out until there is clarification that the site is back up and running. Carefully plan the release of information to all those people who have been concerned about the situation. This will include internal updates to the managers and customer services staff, the communication team so they can be ready for questions at the launch tomorrow, and any stakeholders that are already aware of the problem. Prepare the wording that can be used by the media and shared on social media. It is important to ensure this clarifies the position that it is not a cyber-attack. Be open and transparent about the situation and demonstrate that you responded to people's concerns.

If you are able to directly respond to the original social media posts that highlighted the issue, thank them and make them aware that everything has been returned to normal. If the situation allows you could offer them a voucher or discount as a thank you and recognition from the business. This could be an opportunity to further build brand loyalty by working with customers rather than against them. Continue to monitor for any additional comments or issues, and to ensure that people are aware the situation has been resolved. If further questions emerge, try to answer them honestly and explain what additional action may be taken to protect the website from further problems occurring. Before leaving the situation, consider whether the problem could happen again and whether it should be added to the risk management process. What can you take from the situation and how will it help future issues management? Remember to work with the website and IT team to ensure a process is in place to alert communication staff when website upgrades and developments are going to be put in place. This will allow you to be ready to respond and move quickly if a problem emerges.

Would you have been in a position through your response to inputs 1 and 2 to be able to manage this development? Have you potentially made this a more concerning situation than it has turned out to be? How would you monitor any further problems with the website? What will you do to learn from the experience?

Scenario two

Input 1

The local radio station contacts you to say they have seen inappropriate comments from a senior manager within the business. The employee has a seat at the top table and is closely aligned to the CEO. The manager's comments are derogatory to staff and were posted in an open Facebook group. In the posts they also are dismissive of other senior managers, claiming that they are 'not up to the job'. This is not something that has been picked up by the social media monitoring that exists within the business, and the senior manager is not someone that you have had many dealings with in the past. Your relationship with the local radio station is fairly good but the reporter that has contacted you is new and not someone you have spoken with before. They have given you a deadline to reply in five hours.

WHAT WOULD YOU DO?

The starting point is to try to ensure that regardless of how the issue progresses you build a working relationship with the new reporter. You are likely to work with them in the future, so it is important to use this interaction as a way of laying the foundations for a positive future. But remember that they have a story and will want to use this to show that they are a valuable new employee for the radio station. They may be uncooperative to a direct approach asking them to delay using the story or to stop pursuing it. Whatever develops keep interactions with the journalist friendly and professional even if you end up disagreeing about the outcome.

It is vital to find out as much as possible about the posts, when they were used, where they were shared, and who had a chance to see them. The journalist can provide crucial details that will allow you to do more analysis of the issue. Try to obtain screenshots or images of the posts so that you can attempt to verify that they are from the senior manager and do relate to their current employment. Never assume anything and always check that the information is as it is presented by any news reporter. Once the information has been gathered from the journalist and from your own sources assess it for potential impact on the individuals involved and the business. Employers have a duty of care to their employees, and this should always feature in the decision making. For example, if the person posting comments is going through a traumatic personal situation and may be vulnerable this may change the approach taken to the situation.

The situation needs to be raised with the appropriate people internally. There may be a professional standards and disciplinary issue to be investigated and the relevant staff within HR or legal need to be alerted to the issue. They will also be able to provide valuable advice about the legal position and employment policies and procedures. The timing of any statement that is given to the radio station would need to be carefully managed to allow internal processes to be put in place. No employee should learn of a media article about them at the last minute or without adequate support being put in place. Regardless of the rights and wrongs of the situation, being featured in the news in these circumstances will have a negative impact on an employee. Ensure that someone tells the employee what has happened and what is being done to respond. Speaking to the CEO about the issue is important once there is a clear understanding of what has happened and there is a suggested plan for how to deal with it.

Deadlines are important and should not be ignored. When trying to manage such situations with the media, make people within the business aware of the time pressure on understanding the situation and putting the plan in place. You may, if you have positive relationships, be able to negotiate an extension to the deadline given but it will come at a price. Journalists will always be expecting a more detailed response and possibly the opportunity to ask further questions. Radio stations require voices, and someone may need to speak to represent the business as part of this trade-off. At this point in time there are many ways that the situation could develop, so understanding the details of the situation is the vital first step.

Would you have taken some action before the full picture was known? Did you give a brief statement to the journalist saying this was an internal matter? Was there a different course of action that you would take?

Input 2

Your research shows that the statement was in an open Facebook group that was used by friends of the manager. There are two other managers that are in the group, but they have not liked or commented on the posts. In reality, there are two main posts that are negative about other managers in the business, although no employees are named. HR and legal have given a view that it does breach the company's social media policy that all staff have to agree to. But it is not serious enough to warrant any further investigation. The member of staff who posted them has been spoken to and accepted that they did it when they were angry and upset about a number of things both inside and outside work. They have apologized for the impact of their actions. The company is planning to work with the manager to provide support with the issues they have raised and to reinforce the standards that are required from employees. You have not yet spoken to the CEO, and it is unclear if they have been made aware of the issue and the potential media coverage. The deadline given by the journalist is just two hours away. No further problems have been identified by special social media monitoring put in place to highlight comments around the issue.

WHAT WOULD YOU DO?

Given the details you have of the situation now is the time to develop a communication plan that includes how to escalate the response. When developing the plan consider how a news report about the situation would appear, what it would focus on, and what it could mean to the business, its reputation and other employees. If the impact is rated as low, then a very short statement to minimize the severity of the situation may be all that is required. However, if the report is going to put the CEO and the reputation of the business in a difficult place, a more proactive response will be required. Work through the scenarios and develop the narrative about the situation. The statement may explain that the employee has apologized and is being supported by the organization. It may add that internal feedback can be given through processes that are in place, which will demonstrate an openness and ensure it does not appear defensive. The narrative will depend on the content of the messages and how seriously the posts are viewed.

The aim at this point is to minimize any impact on the business but more importantly on any employee. This should be a story of limited interest that can be contained if it is aired on the radio. It is time to approach the CEO about what has happened and what is being done. When you approach the CEO have the details to hand and talk through the recommended approach and how it can be developed if necessary. This briefing should include a suggested statement to be given to the journalist and also highlight to those involved that detailed social media and media monitoring will remain in place. The CEO needs to be supportive of the approach being recommended because of the connection they have to the employee and the possible additional communication that may be required in relation to what they know and what they have or have not done. The plan needs to identify social media statements to use, internal communication that may be necessary either overtly through the intranet or through briefing key managers, and any stakeholder communication that should be in place. Consider what is required in each of these using the decision-making process identified in Chapter 7 as well as knowledge of previous issues and incidents.

Once all this has been outlined and agreed, contact the reporter to discuss the response and try to gather details of how they are going to report the story. Meet the deadline and be clear that this may mean there are some unknown elements to the situation. Discuss with the reporter the situation and the organization's response to it. If you really need more time, try to move the deadline or request additional time to ensure a more thorough response. Discuss whether they are going to still run the story and if so, if they are going to name the manager who posted the comments. Explain that the employee is being supported and find out about the personal detail that will be given. In some situations, the reporter may decide not to run the story, but if there is a third party upset about what has been said, or other employees commenting, it becomes a more significant story. The information about what will or will not be broadcast needs to be given to the manager who posted the comments alongside relevant support being put in place. If the issue is of minor impact keep the response to a written statement. However, should it be more serious, with a potential investigation, consider having someone senior to voice the statement for the radio reporter. This demonstrates openness and transparency from the organization. Monitor the media and social media to assess whether further action from the escalation plan is required in the coming hours and days.

Did you put support in place for those affected by this situation and the possible radio article? Could you negotiate and influence the journalist to have the personal details removed from the broadcast? Would you have waited to develop a plan until more was known?

Scenario three

Input 1

The business is known for being risqué with its branding and advertising. The marketing manager has been working with an external advertising agency to develop a new campaign to promote the latest product. It was shared with focus groups as part of the development process and while it was supported by the majority there was a small group that disliked it. They were few in number, but their feelings against it were strong. Despite the points they made it was agreed to progress with the advertising approach which is planned to be used on billboards, on social media and on television. The advert has just started to appear on billboards and social media monitoring identifies growing dislike of the message. An anti-advert group has been established on social media and has only limited followers and impact at the moment, but they are starting to tag key journalists into their posts. They have also posted that billboard adverts have been, and will be, vandalized. When you check with the advertising agency, they are not clear how many, if any, have been affected. At the moment there are only 50 sites where the advert is in place. There have been no calls or questions from the news media at this point and with the exception of the marketing manager and team no one within the organization is aware of the situation.

WHAT WOULD YOU DO?
The starting point is to understand the advertising campaign in detail, where it has been circulated, and how long it is going to run. Difficult decisions will have to be made looking at whether to halt the campaign or even to pull it completely. Gathering as much information as

possible is vital and that includes understanding the process that was used to get the advert to completion. In particular, understand who authorized it and whether all the appropriate approvals were given. There may have been a procedural breach or an occasion where someone pushed ahead with the campaign without authorization. Alternatively, it may have been a failure to understand all the perspectives and views about the advertising approach. It is important to ensure that if there has been a procedural problem it is not allowed to overshadow the other actions required to manage the situation. What matters is how people feel about the advert and why they are angry about it. Focusing on a failure in your processes is looking in the wrong place for the communication response.

The next step is to take time to understand who is angry and why. What part of the advert has caused alarm or offence or is felt to be inappropriate? Has it disproportionately affected a section of the community? Use social media information but not just data; take a moment to read and try to fully understand the sentiments that are being posted. Gather details from the advertising agency about how many billboards have been vandalized, what they look like, and what locations they are in. Be quick to remove or respond to vandalized billboards; if they are left in place it may damage people's views of the brand. Be aware that the police may investigate criminal damage so be clear whether or not it has been reported and if something is being done with that information. It is also vital to take the information you have to a senior manager quickly to make those at the top of the business aware of the problem. The information you gather is essential to the decision making.

Would you have immediately ceased running the advertising? Did you halt any of the social media posts? Have you enquired about the television advertising and if it is due to run soon? Is there another course of action you would have taken?

Input 2

The anger about the advert is centred around concerns that it is seen to be negative towards a specific group. The wording on the advertising has caused outrage as it is seen to be out of touch with the current acceptable standards. It is clear that the protests are continuing to grow. Senior managers from across the business including the CEO are being tagged into the growing online posts complaining about the advert and demanding that it is removed. The advertising agency have stopped any additional promotion of the campaign pending a decision on what action the business wants to take. The media are now becoming aware and are asking for comment, including about the cost of the advertising campaign. They have spoken to the anti-advert group who have expressed anger, as well as upset people saying they are offended by the advert.

WHAT WOULD YOU DO?

A crucial decision needs to be made and quickly. It is clear that regardless of the unintentional nature of the offence caused, it is still causing upset and that cannot be ignored. Regardless of the facts of the process undertaken to authorize the advert, the impact it has had may threaten the business's reputation. Looking at the decision-making process now will assist, but swift action needs to be taken before the protests increase further. The advice given to those at the top of the business should be to halt and withdraw the advert to prevent further offence being caused. This can be a positive step showing that the business is listening, is genuinely concerned about what has happened, and is looking to review the situation before moving forward. In addition, find a way to connect with those who have been upset, and the community that is affected, and listen to their issues. This can assist with the revision to the campaign and to future campaign development. Ensure that such action is not seen as a publicity stunt but is a genuine way to understand the impact of the situation on key groups. If the level of protest is significant then a well-prepared CEO can support communication by speaking publicly in an authentic way and addressing the concerns.

Developing the communication plan for the conclusion and with-drawal of the campaign should be approached as an opportunity to build confidence back in the business. It is a chance to demonstrate that this is an open business that will listen and learn. With all the activity developed it is vital to avoid appearing defensive or trying to justify the process by which the advert was created. There is a need to review the way advertising is created to ensure it understands the sensitivities that may exist, but this is an internal matter and not something to focus on externally. A series of questions and answers should be developed to manage any issues that are raised to staff. Share the message from the business across all channels and ensure that employees are aware of what has happened and what to say about it if they are approached by someone. Finally, consider how to move forward and what opportunities exist to involve people in the development of campaigns in the future. How can focus groups be more effectively managed? Demonstrate contrition and a willingness to change in all the communication on the subject. Such situations can cause a significant impact in a short space of time, but with swift action that demonstrates an understanding of the upset and desire by the business to learn and move forward it can be prevented from running over a longer period of time.

Would you have continued to run the campaign? Would you have attempted to justify the position and how the advertising was developed? Did you return to old systems and processes without learning any lessons?

Scenario four

Input 1

A change is made to a product that has been produced the same way for many years. It has been updated to widen its appeal and also make savings for the business. Production costs are reduced and as it was seen as a minor amendment no publicity was put in place ahead of the change. There has been no public recognition of the change that has been made but an email has been received by customer services. It states that the customer is unhappy with the new product and has noticed the change. Far from being a minor adjustment they feel it is a fundamental change to what was a firm favourite. They are claiming they are going to start a campaign to boycott the product and demand that it is returned to its original format. There is no specific demand made within the email.

WHAT WOULD YOU DO?

This may be a one-off complaint that amounts to nothing, or you could be at the start of a rocky road of protest that gains support and puts pressure on the business; it is important to assess the situation carefully. Often different parts of an organization may receive contact so it may be that you have not seen other complaints but that they exist somewhere in the business. Review whether there has been any comment on social media. It is helpful to look at the sales figures and identify any trends that may be emerging. Do the latest figures show sales dropping and could it be linked to the change? Gathering all this information is vital when a problem first appears. Find out if the change is permanent or if it is temporary with a view to gathering feedback before deciding. All this information is critical before ever considering replying to the initial email with anything but an acknowledgement that it has been received.

Would you have taken more action at this early stage? Did you contact the product development team to discuss the situation? Does anyone else in the business need to be involved at this early stage?

Input 2

A reply has been sent thanking the complainant for the feedback but explaining why the change was made and that it is not being reconsidered. There was no further response from the complainant but there have been five further similar letters and emails in the past two weeks. Social media monitoring has been in place since the first complaint was made and now a #boycott of the product is starting to gain support. The issue of the change being made in a covert way is prompting some conspiracy commentary and misinformation about the product and the company. There have now been a small number of questions asked by local news journalists who have become aware of the boycott hashtag. They are asking for details of the change, why it was made, and importantly why it was never communicated to customers.

WHAT WOULD YOU DO?

This highlights the importance of communication being involved in discussions about organizational developments at an early stage. Managing this change could have been carefully planned, which would have reduced the likelihood of customers feeling ignored or that something is being hidden. The communication team would also have been able to assist in carefully wording the reply to the complainant. In addition, customer services teams and those replying could have received training to ensure they understood the implications of the wording used in any response. But with the position that is faced, a key decision needs to be made about how critical the change is to the future of the business, and whether there is any likelihood that growing pressure could force a rethink. If that situation is possible then the issue could be concluded by returning to the original product composition. However, if it is a critical change and has brought significant benefits to the business then a proactive communication plan should be developed. This would focus on clearly explaining not just the benefits to the business but more importantly the benefits to the customer. Find customers who are positive about the change if you can and use their stories or other third parties to help promote the change. Promote these voices within the media and social media.

The situation has escalated and the #boycott is now threatening the business. It is important to establish effective monitoring of social media and to gather relevant data to assist in looking at the way forward. In many cases threats to boycott products do not amount to a significant reduction in sales and disappear as quickly as they arrive. The communication plan needs to take account of this and to look at what would trigger an increase in communication activity. In the short term the narrative about the change needs to be developed so it can be used proactively with the media and on social media.

There may be an opportunity to bring people together to review the position, make suggestions about further developments of the product, and show the business is listening to customer feedback. Within the response, tackling the conspiracy commentary and misinformation needs to be carefully handled. The points need to be categorized and understood. Look at which points are related to the product and which to the company. How much interest have they received? Where necessary a correction should be made and in the worst cases the social media provider alerted to the problem posts and accounts; the legal team may even be spoken to about possible legal action.

Carefully managing this with the local media and with the online protestors can prevent it escalating and avoid the need for further communication or an embarrassing climb down by the business. If a successful conclusion is reached, this situation can be a useful case study internally to demonstrate the points where effective communication could have limited the development of the situation.

Input 3

The interest in the change has almost disappeared. The attempt at a boycott never happened and despite a small number of complaint letters there has been no additional commentary on the matter. The local media have run the story and are no longer interested. There is also no plan to make any further changes to the product for the foreseeable future. But a small group of people are still angry about what has happened and are still making regular posts on social media. You have now found a dedicated Facebook group that has become the central focus of the ongoing social media campaign. The page has a small number of highly active participants but on inspection is saying nothing more than has already been shared.

WHAT WOULD YOU DO?

At this point you could move to social media monitoring and disregard any further proactive communication. The interest in the story has waned and it is only the small group that is now a problem for the business. Consider whether any direct communication has been made to the group to attempt to move the conversation forward. This may be offering to listen to them, inviting them into the company to meet someone senior, or something similar. You may receive a cold response, but it can be the starting point in finding a way to work with the group. The monitoring is important to ensure that there is no sudden escalation in the situation, and to track any new claims that may be made and need to be responded to. Remember to review what has happened and identify where you may be able to make changes to improve the response. It is vital to continue to ensure that there is no long-lasting impact on the reputation of the business from this situation. If reputation is tracked then analyse it for any changes over this period, and if this tracking does not happen consider undertaking it either during or after the problem has occurred and been addressed. Any future changes or product developments should be accompanied by a detailed communication plan to avoid such situations happening in future.

Would you have ignored the complaints? Is this a matter for communication or should customer services have been left to handle the situation? How can you use the case to push for more involvement from communication at a strategic level?

Scenario five

Input 1

A key journalist you speak to regularly has obtained a report that details an extensive list of CEO and senior manager expenses that have been claimed over the past three years. This comes at a time when frontline workers have been reduced by 20 per cent as part of cost-cutting measures announced by the business over a month ago. The journalist is asking for clarification on whether the expenses are accurate and for more detail on what they were. Currently they only have broad headings such as travel, hospitality, etc. The report was provided to the media by an anonymous source, and the journalist is not giving any further detail. The report is accurate and is an internal document that was only accessible to a small group of senior employees. When the cost-cutting measures were announced there was a lot of anger among employees and their families. The media covered the position extensively and the CEO was interviewed giving an explanation about the challenging financial position that the company had found itself in.

WHAT WOULD YOU DO?

When the announcement was made about the cost-cutting measures and redundancies, the communication plan should have considered the ongoing scrutiny that the company would find itself under. It should have provided details of how to approach such scenarios as information being leaked that would challenge the position outlined by the CEO. But if this has not happened the situation can still be turned around by looking in detail at the information that the journalist has. Review the report and be clear what the expenses were for and who they relate to. Statistics can be used in many different ways to say different things so it may be that aspects of the report have been taken out of context. If that is the case, then correcting this position becomes a central part of the narrative used in the response. It may also be possible to use the working relationship with this journalist to provide them with a more detailed explanation or even a briefing to ensure there is clarity about what the figures actually mean. But there may still be some expenses that would not pass public scrutiny given the financial position that the company is now in. The response needs to avoid being too strident and should recognize the difficult position that many in the organization will now be in as they face redundancy.

In developing the approach to the communication, consider what will be said and how it will be said to employees if the story is run. Consider how the situation may escalate further when the story is published or broadcast. Be clear who the voices are opposing the organization in the media coverage; these may be the unions, those made redundant, local politicians, shareholders or other stakeholders. For those stakeholders and shareholders you work with, provide them quickly with a clear position from the business so that they are briefed ahead of any contact by the journalist. Develop a stakeholder management plan to support the longer-term communication on the changes to the business. This can assist in managing the impact of this media story. Be clear on the timescales for the story to be published or broadcast so that internal messages can be shared, and stakeholders contacted with the business's position before it becomes public.

The CEO, if possible, should make the statement and respond to the accusations that are being made. This requires them to be carefully trained so that they are able to be honest and open in their approach and to show empathy and authenticity. Consider how well they can achieve this and in what format they perform better. Communication and media training is about so much more than the words that are used. It is about how they are said, tone and intonation as well as the body language that the interviewee exhibits. If the CEO is not able to be the spokesperson, then ensure they make a statement in the initial stages before using another senior manager for interviews if necessary.

Would you have avoided making a public statement? Have you spoken to HR and legal about the employment position? Is there further communication you would have focused on?

Input 2

Before the journalist runs the story with an explanation from the business about the expenses which are all seen as legitimate, the CEO has received a letter which has been copied to the journalist. It is from a member of staff who says they are a whistle-blower and wants to highlight inappropriate behaviour within the organization. They infer that the current financial situation is due to mismanagement. However, they do not make any direct accusations of illegal activities by anyone in the business. They talk of a 'toxic culture' within the business and claim that employees live in fear that they will lose their jobs. There has been no contact yet by the journalist in relation to the letter but as it has only been received in the post today it is likely it will arrive in the newsroom office today or tomorrow. You have already outlined a plan which details the CEO's position, the media interviews that will be provided, internal and stakeholder communication. All the points have been agreed by the senior team and are ready to go.

WHAT WOULD YOU DO?

Despite a complete communication plan being created it is now time to reassess the approach in light of this development. Whistle-blowers have legal protection in many countries and will usually gain public support in what is seen as a 'David and Goliath' situation. The whistle-blower is the underdog and that attracts sympathy and support, whereas highly paid CEOs do not. Be aware of what legal protections are in place and also what company policies exist around whistle-blowers and how they are approached. The legal department will want to review the letter sent to the CEO to consider the implications it may have, and any redress that could be sought. Communicators would benefit from understanding both the legal position as well as the situation regarding whistle-blowers. From a communication approach, it is important not to get into a public battle with former or current employees.

This is not a time to be defensive as it will be seen as backing up the comments from the whistle-blower. It can impact on the confidence people have in the business. As the letter is likely to be received shortly, consider providing a detailed briefing for the journalist about the position the business is in and how it is looking to develop and return to growth. This could become an opportunity to be open and provide a more rounded picture of what is taking place rather than becoming a battle with an employee. The position regarding the expenses is clear and the communication now needs to expand to look at the operation of the business as a whole.

If you work in a regulated industry the whistle-blower may speak to the regulator, which could lead to further investigations of the allegations. It may also lead to an employment tribunal involving the individual. Both of these will keep the situation running for much longer, which means keeping a constant watch on what is being said, alleged and commented on to consider if any response is necessary.

There needs to be careful scenario planning to review all the options and look at what communication can be prepared and the approach that would be taken. In the short term, once this article has run in the local media you can expect there may be additional questions and requests for interview from national, international and specialist media. Be clear how you will manage these and who will respond on behalf of the business. If you are speaking to international media, consider whether there is someone who can conduct the interview in the required language to avoid the need for a translator or a reliance on subtitles. With the specialist media, be prepared for more searching questions about the past, present and future of the business. Where possible be as helpful as you can with an aim to secure balanced media coverage.

Do you understand the protections that a whistle-blower has? Would you look to hide behind the legal situation? Is there more that you could do to prevent the need for employees to go public to get their point of view heard?

Input 3

The story runs in the local media and the CEO provides a positive response about the work the business is doing. They also recognize the difficult position that some employees are experiencing and commit to do everything possible to help people either to remain in the business or to find new employment. The report includes details that an external inquiry will take place looking at the details the whistle-blower has raised about the culture of the organization. There is a commitment to change and learn wherever possible. There has been a small amount of interest from other media organizations. Shareholders and stakeholders have received communication and no additional issues have been raised. But a small group of ex-employees are now becoming vocal on social media supporting the whistle-blower's comments. They are posting every day and are tagging in local journalists. Everything they are saying has already been addressed in the initial media coverage. They have less than 100 followers at this stage but some of their followers are journalists and local politicians.

WHAT WOULD YOU DO?

In the short term, do nothing and monitor the operation of the group. Review how it develops and whether it gathers any more followers. Consider what they are saying and assess whether there is anything new within it. But as they are ex-employees and may have an issue with the business it is likely that any direct response to the posts will spark an angry reply. This monitoring and assessment may need to continue for some time, or until there is another planned announcement about the business or the planned review. In the interim time the proactive communication work of the business still needs to continue. But announcements should be assessed to ensure it is not going to trigger a response or to prepare for it if a reaction is expected. The operation of the business needs to continue but the communication plan must be reviewed and considered on a regular basis. It should include details of what would trigger a change in approach or a direct response to the group posting on social media.

Would you have attempted to contact the ex-employees? How would you look to move forward with communication? Are you developing a long-term communication plan to deal with the ongoing discussion and the outcome of the investigation?

KEY LEARNING POINTS

- Assess each situation quickly but as thoroughly as possible. Recognize the gaps that you may have in understanding so that you can factor it into the decision-making process.

- Ensure internal governance systems are in place to allow situations to be escalated and to provide frontline staff with important information that they may need to use with customers or the public.

- Taking an honest and open approach to issues management will lead you on the right path to secure an effective outcome. Try to hide or minimize the severity and impact of situations and you risk a backlash.

- Be prepared to be flexible in your approach. Consider how you will respond if the situation escalates and be ready to react.
- It is important for all the communication team to be involved in working through scenarios and considering the steps to take, when to escalate action, and how to bring a satisfactory conclusion.

Conclusion

Such scenarios as have been outlined in this chapter could be faced by any organization at any point in time. Some will develop and become critical situations and others will have only limited impact. The key within all the scenarios that have been considered is that communication needs to be involved in the discussion about the operational response both to advise and to listen. Communicators have a key role to play and can act as a bridge between the public and journalists and those running the business. Building trust and confidence in the communication team and staff is vital for that moment when problems and issues emerge. They should be honest with the CEO and top team about how the situation looks, what may happen, and how they can proactively approach communication. Leadership needs to be supportive of the communication plan that is detailed and work to support it. The advice and guidance communicators give can make the difference between an issue that grows and one that is managed and curtailed. The scenarios also highlight the importance of having a plan, looking at future developments and being ready to adapt to emerging situations. All these are critical to managing issues.

Decision making is important to responding to any developing problem. Being able to make effective decisions while under pressure from time constraints and internal demands is fundamental to an effective response. There will be moments when the right choice limits the situation so even if the first decision does not have the right result there will be further chances to intervene positively. In each case discussed here, gathering as much data and information as possible and then analysing it is essential as the foundation before considering the action to take and the decisions to make. Building structures and frameworks that can assist the communicator to move quickly through the analysis and assessment is vital. Once systems are in place the next step is working through scenarios to discuss the actions to take, and to build knowledge and experience among the communication team.

10

Bringing things together and what to take away

Introduction

Managing issues is an everyday occurrence for communicators no matter where they work or who they are working with. Doing it well and getting better results is only possible if we take a step back and reflect on what we are doing, how we are doing it and what the outcomes have been. Effective issues management is essential for all businesses and organizations; without it, attention will be distracted from core business due to teams being drawn into dealing with many critical incidents and crises. If action is taken at an early enough stage this effort can be directed into what really matters to the business. Leaving issues and failing to assess and consider acting is like a lottery where you hope that the situation does not develop and impact further on the business. Getting these things right matters. It matters because you can prevent losses both financial and reputational. It matters because it can allow you to build a reputation, maintain investment, secure market share and grow and build. There are always opportunities that arise when issues and problems are being considered. There are opportunities to demonstrate the values of the business, to prioritize support to customers and service users, and to build confidence from diverse groups.

Communicators are not the only people who are central to the issues management process. There are individuals and teams across the business that need to understand both how to recognize an emerging problem and also how to support the response. The information within this book has been produced primarily for those working in communication roles but should also be able to assist anyone faced with tackling a growing issue. Small business owners and single-person businesses may lack the finances to engage communication professionals to undertake this work. The processes, principles and approaches that are outlined can underpin issues management for all organizations no matter how big or small. What matters is that you recognize there is an issue that needs to be resolved and you are ready to take some form of action to address it.

The starting point

It is critical to have ways the business can identify problems at an early stage and at a point before they have become so big that they are a significant threat. The earlier the intervention can be considered, and a course of action decided upon, the more likely a satisfactory conclusion will follow. Waste time and introduce unnecessary delays and the moment to act will have drifted away from you. All this is not just something that the communication team alone have to be focused on. The whole business needs to be alert to problems that may develop and be ready to come together to address them. Having a structure in place that involves all parts of the business will ensure situations can be discussed quickly and action plans prepared. Such structures should not be limited to responding to emergencies and crises and can play a broader role in supporting organizations with issues management. The framework should encourage every section of the business to feel able to highlight problems and this includes the communication team. But effective issues management is about more than structures, procedures and frameworks – it needs the right culture to be in place. This is a culture of 'no blame' where issues can be highlighted without the fear that those raising them will be sidelined, punished or disciplined in some way.

The right people from teams across the business should be brought together regularly to discuss issues and how they are managed. This can be part of the risk management systems and can be used to help build knowledge, skills and experience of dealing with issues. The more discussions around how to deal with situations can take place on a regular basis, the more alert people will be to potential situations. Communicators have a vital role to play in this work and should be confident in stepping forward to both raise concerns about situations and provide plans detailing how to respond. It means the communication team must feel ready and able to stand up and speak out. Continuous professional development for all communicators should include issues management and crisis response. Even before the global Covid-19 pandemic emerged in early 2020 there was a need for communicators to be ready to deal with challenging situations. Since that time everyone has been affected by this worldwide crisis and the importance of effective issues management has grown. It needs to be part of every communicator's skillset.

Structures are important but there are other ways to support the work to manage issues that should be considered. Communication teams need to ensure that as well as having the skills required, they have access to the right systems and technology in place to make identifying, managing and evaluating issues easier. There needs to be a comprehensive social media monitoring system in place as this will play a key role in both identifying problems and developing responses. Media monitoring also needs to be in place covering online news sites, radio, television and physical newspapers. Databases or ways to log issues, plans, and media responses are also important to the management of issues. Being able to track problems is essential and allows the communicator to be able to respond as outlined in an escalation plan. It also ensures the team is connected and able to recognize developing situations. Technology is a key way to support the management of everyday issues. Once these structures and systems are in place and used on a daily basis, they can be brought in quickly to support the response when pressure starts to mount. If there is a reluctance among leaders to fund the required databases and systems that communicators need, they should be shown the positive impact that they can have on the response. But if that fails, try to identify no-cost alternatives that will include social media alerts and alerts linked to online news sites. Leaders in organizations may need to see the organizational impact that poor responses can have to provide the required finances. Try to push your case so that you have access to the necessary tools.

The role of media and social media

Communicators work with news media and social media on a daily basis. They are primary ways of sharing positive stories about the organization to customers and the public. Existing systems will be in place to ensure the effective use of them, from developing relationships with key journalists through to promoting social media channels. They have become such a central part of the work that is done that people may not have analysed how they are used and how this could be improved. Stepping away from the frontline of communication delivery to conduct this assessment is a huge challenge. But doing this work will ensure a more effective response to issues. Review your relationships with journalists and the networks that you have available. Consider where the gaps may be and actively build new relationships where necessary as well as maintaining existing ones. Alongside this the social media plan and operation should be reviewed to ensure it is still supporting the key requirements of the business. Understand how media and social media work most effectively within your day-to-day communication activity.

Monitoring matters

Monitoring is an essential part of everyday communication. It is critical that a close watch is kept on what is said and published that relates to the business. The aim is to ensure that whenever something important is said it is identified and considered in case there is any impact on the business. This requires the use of keywords, phrases, areas and subjects that are of interest or may be connected to the business. Having effective search parameters in place can mean the difference between finding that complaint about the business and missing it. This monitoring should take place every day but be able to scale up when necessary and be more closely scrutinized when an issue or situation has emerged and is being actively managed. Consider investing in training and equipment that will support the communication team undertaking this work. Remember there may not be a specialist social media team or media management team in place. Everyone in the team needs to be ready and able to review the monitoring of both the media and social media. This will increase the alert level within the communication team. Understanding the processes for both media and social media management will allow the response to an issue to proceed more quickly.

Remain alert

Be alert and ready for the moment when an issue is identified through the monitoring that takes place. Have systems that people can use, because no one can remain alert for 100 per cent of the time; these systems and processes will support you to swiftly recognize that something of note is happening. In addition, training can support people, including communicators, to know what they are looking for and how to identify it. There is always a chance that an issue slips past us and begins to develop but with the right training even those situations that pass you by will be spotted before they become a significant issue. For those who are new to communication this training is critical but even the more experienced communicators can benefit from refining their skills. Part of the alert phase is also to understand what may happen with a developing problem. This means looking at what has happened to other businesses, considering good practice as well as understanding local communities, customers and employees.

Understand networks

Really get to understand those in your network and where the business has connections both across social media and with the media. Know the journalists that carefully follow what the business does, those who may have a passing interest, and those who may have a history of producing negative stories about the organization. In the same way communicators should conduct stakeholder mapping, the communicator can also do this for the news media. There will also be journalists and news outlets that you would like to develop closer working relationships with, and these should also be identified. With social media it is vital to understand who the key influencers are, which accounts may be problematic to the business, and what social media networks have the most impact on your reputation. Understanding the details of both media and social media connections will allow effective targeting of your communication and help maximize the impact of your response.

Review decision making

Respond to an emerging situation by using the media and social media stakeholder mapping to assist your decision making. As outlined in Chapter 7, be clear how you will be effective in decision making and how you will limit the impact of any biases:

- Do not just use intuition and a 'gut feeling' to decide on what action should be taken and where communication should be focused, either in news media or social media.
- Discuss and outline your options within that decision-making process; articulating them clearly will assist in defining the next steps.
- Be aware of challenges that you may face and be clear how you will respond.

This should be part of the escalation plan for the issue. Consider future scenarios, how things may develop, and how social media and news interest may evolve. This can then inform the options for action that are put in place.

It is not just for those with expertise in media and social media to undertake this work and be aware of the steps that need to be taken. Managers and communication leaders should have the necessary skills and training to be able to define the approach and be ready to develop and adapt it as required. Leaders will not be undertaking all the tactical work, but they should be able to direct others to follow the four-step process and know how to assess the results of any action. Speed is not the only thing that matters when managing issues and problems. Thorough and detailed understanding of the situation from all perspectives is essential.

Stakeholders and relationships

Throughout the book there has been detailed consideration of the role of stakeholder management and building effective relationships. This remains at the core of effective day-to-day communication both when managing problems and promoting the business. It is critical to the success of dealing with issues and limiting any impact on the reputation of the business. Understanding people and how they may respond will provide valuable insight to any communication plan. Developing this understanding comes from listening, researching, and building effective conversations on a daily basis. It is easy to lose sight of how important this is when communicators are under pressure to keep delivering activity.

Where possible this listening can develop into involving people in the running and decision making within the business. Providing different perspectives and challenging an accepted narrative around a situation is more easily done for those who are outside the business. For example, the business may be working with an influencer to promote products and services. On the face of it there are no particular problems involving the influencer, and all legal checks have presented no concerns. But the head of a charity you work with regularly has criticized some of the comments that the influencer has made in the past. This insight could lead you to reassess the decision to work closely with the influencer and may also present early identification of an issue that may emerge if you continue. This level of detailed consideration is critical for significant decisions that are driving the business and are affecting its reputation.

Building business confidence

Effectively working with others and opening up the business are not as easy as they may first appear. It requires a confidence within the business, to be able to listen to others and consider points even where there is disagreement. It also necessitates a communicator having additional skills to support this work. The ability to influence effectively and ethically and to create connections is essential. These are often seen as 'softer' skills but can bring the biggest results for any organization. A communicator who is skilled at communication will be able to achieve a lot, but to go that bit further they need to be able to operate at a senior level, understand the language of the business, and be effective in influencing both within and outside the organization. It can mean the difference between an angry stakeholder concerned that they have not been aware of a problem that has emerged, and a stakeholder that is able to support the response to the emerging issue.

Developing maps

Stakeholder management is a fundamental part of effective communication for organizations. Having stakeholder maps that can be used in response to specific circumstances will assist the communication response. Mapping is important for all day-to-day communication, not just when dealing with an issue. If this work is not already in place, then spend some time on developing it so that it can be called upon for issues management and crisis communication work. Know the following:

- Who are the stakeholders?
- Where are they based?
- How do they like to get their information?
- What do they want to know?
- Who should be the person to contact them?

Within this work it is important to identify the stakeholders who require updates on the management of an issue, and those who will want to be involved in the discussions and decision making. For example, if your business has a number of investors and within that group there are two who are keen to be more involved in the business, then they may be contacted to provide a perspective on actions being taken to manage an issue. But other investors may just want to have an email update about the problem and what is being done to manage it. This highlights why it is important to carefully map stakeholders and do a deep dive within the categories that you identify. Know your stakeholders in as much detail as possible.

The work with stakeholders and key groups cannot be something that happens at one point in time and then never revisited. New people will join the business and the communication team, new stakeholders will emerge, and new relationships will need to be forged. Review your stakeholder mapping on a regular basis. It is often useful to put a date in the diary every three months to review whether the stakeholder mapping and plans are still effective and useful, and to update them if required. Any substantial change within the business or that impacts on the business such as a crisis should also trigger a review of the stakeholder work that is in place. When an issue or problem emerges, it is not the time to try to bring stakeholder mapping up to date as the incident demands a swift response.

The four A's of issues management

Having a process to support the resolution of issues can save time and keep you focused on achieving a positive response. Systems and procedures are important ways to assist the daily management of communication, as we have seen. Following the four A's outlined below can ensure people are prepared and ready to put an effective response in place.

Assess

When a problem emerges or looks likely to emerge, the starting point is to fully assess the situation. This means gathering all the information about what has happened, what was happening before the problem developed, and what may be going to happen. It requires an understanding of the current social and environmental conditions. Gather information on what is known from the past, present and future surrounding the business. The aim is to have as full a picture as possible of both the issue and the context within which it has emerged.

Analyse

Once as much information as possible has been gathered about the situation it is time to review and consider exactly what it means. This analysis is a critical step in issue management as it will guide the decision making and could mean the difference between taking the right action and missing the mark. Consider all the information that you have in front of you and use a decision-making model to assist you in developing the plan. But beware of becoming paralysed in the analysis of the situation. Use the assessment to guide the analysis and help you move forward.

Articulate

The plan will need a clear narrative about the situation. This is the words and images that are used which can reinforce the required position and calm troubled waters. The approach needs to be clear and easy to understand. It must also have honesty and integrity built into the comments; an ethical approach to the communication is critical. Fail to demonstrate an ethical response based on listening and building honesty in the conversation and you risk making the situation worse. Be clear about the messages that will be used during the first interaction and those that may follow if the situation develops.

Act

Once the first three stages have been completed then you should be ready to take action to respond to the emerging issue. The plan should be clear, together with a narrative that underpins the steps that are being taken. At this point the plan should consider how things may develop and escalate and how this may change and develop the communication response. The approach to the issue should be flexible and adaptable though, so that no matter what happens in the initial stages the plan will be able to change and respond as necessary.

The four A's of issues management are supported by developing an escalation plan. This will support the approach that has been outlined and the developments that may be required, which have featured in the Act phase.

Effective incident communication

Using the four A's should aid the creation of an incident communication plan. This plan will detail what is required in the initial stages of the issues management and will be the foundation for any future action. For communicators, it should follow the outline of any regular communication plan and have clear aims and objectives. The narrative or messages around the issue should be carefully detailed so that they can be used as required. The plan will detail the key audiences, which may be a handful of people who have raised concerns about the situation in the first instance but then could be widened to include staff, stakeholders and other groups. What will be done, at what point and by what method should be clearly laid out in an action plan. This includes ensuring there are details of who will be involved in any communication activity that is in place. Finally, no plan should be created that does not include details of how evaluation of the activity will be conducted.

Within the planning there needs to be an escalation plan which details the actions that may be taken when certain circumstances are triggered. More details about this are outlined in the next section. The incident communication plan should also be linked to other plans that exist in relation to the situation that has emerged. If there are response plans, operational plans or other activities that are outlined, the communication should be closely aligned.

Communication has a key role to play in managing and successfully concluding an issue that impacts on the business. Being prepared and having an effective incident communications plan can create confidence in the response and help elevate communication to sit strategically and operate as an adviser to the senior management team.

IN FOCUS

An effective incident communication plan should include all of the following subject areas as a starting point: aim, objectives, narrative, structure/governance for the issue in question, audiences including key stakeholders, monitoring, plan including details of which members of the team will be involved in completing the actions, any resource implications, whether they are staffing or financially related, and evaluation. This would be the basic framework that would then be expanded and developed in line with the details of the issue or incident as it develops. New data and insight will be used to refine and update the plan.

Preparing for developments

The next steps, and what may lie ahead, should be in our minds from the first moment that the issue emerges. Preparing an escalation plan is a way to detail the possible scenarios and how the business will respond should they appear. Having the escalation plan in place can save time by thinking through issues ahead of them emerging and agreeing decisions. This gives the communicator the support to act without using a lengthy approvals process. It will also help to build confidence in the communication approach and management. Senior leaders within the business can feel reassured that the communicator has a detailed knowledge and understanding of the situation as well as having strategic oversight. There is confidence from seeing that future plans have been developed and the situation is being closely monitored. Any senior leaders in the organization will have one less worry on their minds as they know the communication will operate and they will only be brought in when required.

Developing an escalation plan for an issue requires five things to be considered:

1 the history of the issue or situation and understand what and who was involved;

2 what the situation means to the business and to other key connections outside the business;

3 the critical aspects of the issue and how they threaten to affect the business;

4 the impact that the issue has had or threatens to have if it develops;

5 the people who are affected by the issue or who may have something to say about it.

Using all the information gathered within the five steps you can then build a chart or matrix which details the potential future developments and the impact that they may have. If you have any experience of risk management matrices the same approach can be used to help map out the situation that you are dealing with. Consider all the 'what ifs' from the information you have about the issue and detail the communication steps that will be taken. In presenting this information to the organization, use a format that people will understand and have confidence in. This will encourage greater acceptance of the approach being outlined within the leadership team. For example, if you are in a regulated and hierarchical business the strict risk management approach within a spreadsheet may be the most acceptable format. However, if you are in a creative business then a more visual representation of the position and future options would be expected.

Keep learning

Issues and problems occur on a regular basis – for some businesses this may be daily – and each one brings an opportunity to learn and develop. Learning from our own experiences is essential but it is also an elevated risk as no one wants to see things fail in order to boost their own learning. There is a lot to be gained by looking at the problems that other organizations face and reviewing how they respond, particularly focusing on the decisions they make and the actions they take. Expanding our understanding of how we may respond, what paths can be taken, and the impact that decisions may have is vital to growth as a communicator. Whatever way you choose to learn and develop, ensure that it is built into your approach to managing issues and incidents. It should be a cycle of tackling situations and then learning from them to improve how you respond in the future.

Reflection time

Remember to reflect on what you have worked on. Look at the elements that were successful and try to unpick exactly why they worked for the issue that you were addressing. The same approach may not work in the future with a different situation, so understanding why it worked on this occasion is vital to really knowing what you can take forward. Consider what you could have done differently. Perhaps you were slow to respond or did not fully understand the situation that was developing, or the response created additional problems. Whatever occurred, consider how things could have been improved. This time to reflect is critical and should be built into any issues management plan and process within the business. If you have experienced a comparable situation in the past, then use the review time to compare the responses and the outcomes. Understand which approach was more effective and why it may have been successful. It is part of continuously learning and developing as a communication professional.

Evaluating activity

Evaluating the business's current standing within the marketplace, with customers, with staff and with others, is important as a benchmark so the issues management can be assessed for effectiveness. Really understanding the business, what it does, and how it is viewed will support all forms of day-to-day communication work. It helps to define the priorities, identify opportunities and demonstrate the impact of activity. Communicators need to invest time to get to know the business from top to bottom, whether they are working in-house or providing support through an agency. This must include understanding what the existing communication has meant to the reputation of the business. For effective issues management, the communicator must see the impact that acting to address situations has brought and also where inaction has been either beneficial or problematic.

Look at the details

Use all this information that you can gather from developments, previous events, considering the action of others, and from day-to-day communication work to continuously learn and improve the approach to issues management. Consider whether the existing structure and processes are working or need to be refined. Review the issues management plans that you have in place and assess where they could be improved. Identify where there are any gaps in the response and see what is required to address them. This work to learn, develop and review does not have to be done in isolation. Where possible bring in external resources to support the work and provide independent oversight. Often communicators can become too close to a situation and find it difficult to pull back and be more objective. If there are groups you have involved in consultation on aspects of communication, then consider asking them to assess the plan to manage an issue. Alternatively, bring experts in reputation and issues management to review and provide advice about how to develop the approach. This could also be linked to additional training for those who require it within teams.

Rebuilding trust

Even when the management of the issue or incident has not been effective or has escalated outside your control there is still an opportunity to recover and help to rebuild the business by rebuilding trust in it. Start by reviewing what happened with the issue and the management of it, and where communication did or did not make a positive impact. Detail what you have learnt about both the organization and the subject that you are dealing with. This is the foundation of improving and refreshing a corporate communication plan in connection with the issue. Using the key principles of issues management, update the communication activity and focus on building a connection with those who have been the most severely affected. Views and beliefs about the business can be improved by listening and understanding what has happened because of the issue, and then committing to address it.

Communicators need to be clear with those at the top of the business that rebuilding trust is something that cannot be delivered overnight and will require a consistent and focused communication plan and activity. But this push to regain the trust of the public, customers and others will not happen in isolation, and any further issues or incidents that arise could derail this work. It is why developing daily monitoring and assessment of issues and incidents is critical so that swift action can be taken to deal with multiple issues. Rebuilding trust is an active process needing proactive and transparent communication that is supported by leaders and senior managers. Even when an issue has come to a conclusion and is no longer being talked about in the media and on social media, there is still an opportunity to regain any lost trust.

Putting ourselves to the test

Issues and problems can emerge at any point and if the business is not regularly faced with challenges then testing is essential. Testing ensures that the team are ready to respond, know what is expected and can quickly move from daily promotional communication into issues management roles. Make the tests as useful to learning and development as possible, and be realistic about what you may face. Regular testing will provide insight into areas for further development on a team or an individual basis. The test should, where possible, involve other departments within the business to stress test the connections that exist internally.

Testing does not need to involve expensive and time-consuming exercises. A huge amount of information can be gathered by developing a paper-based scenario that you work through as a team. Try to assess all phases of the issues management process on an annual basis to then inform further development that can be included in the training plan. Communicators should be able to:

- identify an emerging problem at an early stage;
- carry out an assessment of the impact of the issue and the potential challenges it could bring;
- develop a communication plan to respond to the issue;
- make decisions quickly with partial information and when under pressure;
- adapt the approach and change the response plan quickly as a situation escalates;
- consider the future impact the issue may have and carry out scenario planning;
- promote issues management, dealing with problems and employees at all levels within the business up to the CEO.

The scenarios outlined in Chapter 9 can help in starting this testing regime, and can help train and educate communicators or those connected to issues management. Gather the relevant people together and ask them to explain how they would deal with each of the inputs as the situation develops. Review what has been covered and where there may be gaps in the approach. Discuss the rationale behind the actions taken and consider what additional steps could be put in place. Be prepared to question your decisions and try to push your thinking. Learning in an almost real situation should help to make the training more relevant.

If the development of scenarios and tests is something you are not confident with then there are ways to access additional external support. Consider working with another organization or business and sharing knowledge and experiences. This may help in considering what has worked and areas that need to be focused upon. However, for businesses this can be problematic as they are in competition with others and can be reluctant to share experiences. In those situations, consider bringing in an issues and reputation management specialist who will be able to review your current approach, plans and processes and develop a training plan including scenario-based tests. They should have experience of working on issues management across industries and businesses that they can use to benchmark your approach. Spending some budget on improving issues management could save the business money in the long term. Potential damage to the reputation of the business will be minimized and communicators will be ready to see how they could turn the situation into an opportunity.

Making issues management a daily affair

Having looked at the training and testing that can assist in managing issues, make sure it is not seen as something that only happens once a year; effective issues management has to be part of daily business. It needs to be something that is considered alongside answering media enquiries, putting content onto social channels, and sending information to employees. There are many reasons people will use to justify why they have not invested time to review and improve their approach to issues management, including:

- a lack of time;
- they feel it is not necessary;
- no one in the business is interested;
- there are no resources for the work;
- management are not supportive.

Justifying why you have not undertaken any work in this area will not help you or the business when the inevitable happens. For every reason not to do this work, there are many more reasons to support active learning about issues management. Effectively dealing with problems, issues and incidents will save you time and money, and protect the reputation of the organization. It will prevent media or social media exposés, avoid costly legal or other proceedings, and allow you more time for the positive promotional work.

There are some simple ways that you can introduce this daily focus on issues management into your work:

1 **Effective monitoring systems**
   Make sure you have a system in place that will both alert you to social media and media coverage of note and will be a source of vital information when managing situations. Use technology and suppliers to support this while also ensuring that the team are trained to understand how to use the information and build it into the response.

2 **Social media responses**
   Have a clear approach to who will respond to comments on social media, when, and how. Ensure there is training and support in place for whoever will be crafting the responses. Do not just leave it to social media specialists; make sure other staff can step in and help to manage social media when an issue is emerging.

3 **Media relationships**
   Build and develop your relationships with journalists. Work with them so they understand the business but also so that communication staff understand how the journalists operate. Help the managers in the business see the benefits that close working relationships with news media bring. Know your key news media, who they are, and what they are interested in.

4 **Know your risks**
   Understanding where the biggest threats to the organization's reputation are will assist when monitoring for emerging issues. It will help not only now but also as you look to potential challenges in the future. Discuss the list of risks regularly so that you can make people aware and ready to act, and ensure new risks are included.

5 Educate others

Ensure the role of communication in managing problems and issues is understood throughout the business. Demonstrate the business benefits that come from effective communication supporting dealing with situations, including financial savings and minimizing reputational damage. Use case studies and examples to support your work. Keep the discussion of issues management on the agenda.

6 Introduce or amend systems

If you have a system to manage issues, then it may be time to review it and ensure it is still fit for purpose. If you do not have a system, then now is the time to put one in place. Look at the areas of concern, consider how you can work with others, and identify the systems that will support your endeavours. This includes having risk management spreadsheets, systems to gather information about 'near misses', and databases to chart the response and its impact.

7 Discuss issues management

Create a meeting structure that will ensure issues management does not get overlooked. This includes sharing good practice, detailing work that has been undertaken and the impact it has had, and developing plans and approaches to manage future issues. The meetings should involve voices from outside the organization, if possible, to challenge ways of thinking.

8 Build resilience

Dealing with a significant issue or a series of smaller issues can take its toll on any communicator. It is easy to feel under attack and to then become defensive in your way of thinking. Test the communication response and the team to help to provide some certainty as to how issues are managed. Continuing to test and discuss situations will provide a foundation to work from. Encourage those involved to increase their resilience to prevent them feeling overwhelmed.

In an uncertain world the communicator needs to be ready to respond to situations that quickly emerge. Today's minor problem can very swiftly be tomorrow's crisis. Businesses can go from profitable and considering growth to facing a battle to survive, with a lack of confidence from customers and investors. The spotlight can suddenly be put on who they are and what they do. This is why the daily management of issues and incidents needs to be front of mind not just for communicators but for managers and the CEO.

What next?

The chances are that as you finish reading this book you will already have a number of issues and potential incidents that you are aware of or dealing with. This is an opportunity to take some elements from the book and put them into immediate use. Consider how you are going to assess the situation and prepare the response. Take time to look at how you are making decisions and what biases may come into play when you are doing so. Review whether there is a robust escalation plan in place to be ready for the way the situation may develop. If you do not have any immediate issues to deal with then you are in a very lucky position. But the time is right to review what you usually do and look at ways to improve your approach.

The details within the book should help to create and improve the systems and processes that are in place. Keep focused on what you need to develop and what works so that there is no waste of effort and energy. Consider streamlining the issues management response to maximize the resources you have available. But do not feel this has to be done in private. Gathering different views and listening to different voices both inside and outside the business will bring the best results. It will allow critical review of the approach and the communication principles including of media and social media management. Bring people in to challenge your thinking and test your approaches to solving problems and issues.

Everyday problems will always affect businesses. They will be happening now, today, tomorrow and in the days, weeks, months and years ahead. From unhappy customers through to inappropriate comments from staff, these moments will test the communicator.

With some planning, preparation and thought we can prevent those everyday problems from becoming long-term reputational failures.

KEY POINTS TO TAKE AWAY

- Create an issue and incident management plan that details the approach you are going to take and how it may develop.
- Be ready to escalate the action you take quickly when it is triggered by a change in circumstances.
- Have a detailed and thorough approach to monitoring both media and social media for emerging problems.
- Ensure there is an organizational policy about how social media is used both by the communication team and by employees.
- Develop plans for the biggest risks but remain alert for other problems that may emerge.
- Remember that communication is not just something that communicators do, and that other employees and stakeholders also have an important part to play.
- Build strong networks and relationships with groups and individuals that are important both to the business and in managing issues.
- Challenge your thinking and the way you approach decision making so that you consider a broad range of options and work to ensure diversity and inclusivity within your approach.
- The communication team is not in this alone. Issues management should involve those at the top of the business and including them is critical.
- Demonstrate the benefits of the communication activity so that you can build confidence from senior management and secure a seat advising at the 'top table'.
- Remember the four A's of issues management – Assess, Analyse, Articulate and Act.

Successfully managing issues can contain damaging situations and build support for the brand or business. The road to improving everyday issues management starts here.

INDEX

From 4 December 2025 the EU Responsible Person (GPSR) is:
eucomply oÜ, Pärnu mnt. 139b – 14, 11317 Tallinn, Estonia
www.eucompliancepartner.com

www.ingramcontent.com/pod-product-compliance
Lightning Source LLC
Chambersburg PA
CBHW041208220326
41597CB00030BA/5097

9 781398 606975